INTRODUCING
FEMINIST PASTORAL CARE
AND COUNSELING

INTRODUCING

FEMINIST PASTORAL CARE AND COUNSELING

Nancy J. Gorsuch

INTRODUCTIONS IN **FEMINIST** THEOLOGY

THE
PILGRIM
PRESS
Cleveland

For David,
most generous life partner

The faith practices listed on pages 8–9 from *Growing in the Life of Christian Faith* are used by permission of the Office of Theology and Worship, Presbyterian Church, U.S.A.

The constructs of a healthy woman listed on pages 75–76 are from Mary Ballou and Nancy W. Gabalac, *A Feminist Position on Mental Health,* 1985. Courtesy of Charles C. Thomas, Publisher, Ltd., Springfield, Illinois.

The Pilgrim Press, 700 Prospect Avenue, E., Cleveland, OH 44115-1100 U.S.A.
pilgrimpress.com

Printed in the United States of America on acid-free paper

06   05   04   03   02   01   5   4   3   2   1

Library of Congress Cataloging-in-Publication Data

Gorsuch, Nancy J., 1951–
    Introducing feminist pastoral care and counseling / Nancy J. Gorsuch.
       p.   cm. – (Introductions in feminist theology)
    Includes bibliographical references and index.
    ISBN 0-8298-1440-X (alk. paper)
       1. Pastoral theology. 2. Feminist theology. 3. Pastoral counseling.   I. Title.
    II. Series.

BV4011.3 .G67 2001
253′.082 – dc21

                                                                  2001041422

Contents

Foreword

In the words of a famous Barbra Streisand song, this text finds the author "putting it all together"—and with a point of view. She offers us a model of what pastoral theological reflection, or, as I prefer, practical theology, might look like when the method is critical dialogue and the concern is "making sense."

The purpose of a foreword is anticipatory, that is, to guide the reader in thinking ahead enough to get as much as possible from the text. So anticipate this: Gorsuch holds five areas of knowledge in critical dialogue with each other and with selected feminist perspectives, focusing upon the thought of Sallie McFague, Sharon Welch, and Rita Nakashima Brock among many others. The knowledge areas are pastoral practice, social location, socio-cultural-political theory, religious traditions, and feminist psychology and therapy. She is clear about her specific selection of resources within each category, so the dialogues remain focused.

These dialogues are to serve the end of informed and creative practice in the areas of pastoral care, pastoral counseling, and pastoral consultation. A pastoral situation reflecting each of those areas extends throughout the text, keeping always before the reader the author's insistence on the ways in which the dialogue leads to a more informed practice.

And this is in the service of a critically reconstructed Reformed theology that will inform and affirm the context of congregations, with full partnership (or, as she prefers, collaboration) of ordained and lay leadership.

I have said that the author puts all of this together—and with a point of view. She recognizes that pastoral practice in all modalities is "thick" and "messy," that is, that it itself discloses a complex and ambiguous human situation where "problems" carry multiple dimensions and complex social and material relations.

But she doesn't get lost there or let go of the complexity and begin solving problems or applying her knowledge to particular pastoral situations. Instead she allows very particular and concrete embodiments of "problems" (that is, specific human situations of personal crisis, marriage difficulties, and a dying church facing its own future) to "ground" her intellectual dialogues. Thus the reader must respond to her invitation to "see" and to "act" with real stuff at hand.

One might say—I am saying—that this is not a problem-solving text, but rather a perspective-shaping text. For when knowledge emerges through dialogue, it will be nuanced in ways that refuse ideological application and invite creativity and imagination. The author speaks of and defines "rhetorical strategies" to guide and explore the various processes and does not allow herself to get away with fixing and solving, or even "marketing" a particular perspective. This may be demanding of you, dear reader, but do "keep your eye on the prize" of what it means to be faithful to particular persons and situations when there are alternative renderings of their possible meanings, and when invitations to change will be heard from within the dynamic complexities of real living. For the author is a feminist with nuanced perspectives, a pastor with a disciplined intellect, a counselor respecting the ordinary complexities of personal existence, and a consultant with the patience and persistence to hear congregational refusals and struggles as well as their possibilities and programs.

If you are patient, the author will guide you along the way. Her central themes are those of faithful response, resistance, and connection, and each is carefully defined and presents her constructive point of view. For example, she reconstructs a Reformed view of God in order to hold on to God's freedom to be present and to act in the midst of pastoral situations. She understands the various processes and dynamics of resistance as sometimes the beginning conditions for ongoing liberation and justice. She speaks of connection rather than community because of her desire to present an understanding of interdependence that doesn't require the loss of self. It is here that the nuances of her feminist thought are most apparent, and that her selected resources are themselves being critiqued and reconstructed. Along with the three pastoral situations, the three themes recur throughout the text and provide its dialogical movement.

The author has not been explicit about the ecclesiology out of which she practices, although the text discloses her interests in collaborative leadership, the cohabitation of care and justice, and an implicit affirmation that "little things count." That is, in our congregations, it is important to listen to one another, to appreciate diversities and multiple meanings, to risk, and, always, to reflect on our pastoral experiences (pastoral work) not only so that they might be grounded and informed theologically, but also so that they themselves might continually urge theological conceptualization to be inclusive of the insights of those working out and embodying their faith in their particular places.

Throughout the text the author refers to the careseeker's "privileged status." Now in the name of the foreword writer's "privileged status," I call your attention to three significant contributions that may slip out of this text's significance unless underlined.

First is her recognition that congregations themselves are "caregivers" and "careseekers." I argue that it is care and mission that constitute congregation, and not that congregations "do" programs of care and mission. Gorsuch recognizes that it is time for pastoral care practitioners to be competent and available to consult with congregations as they strive and struggle to make decisions about who they are and can be. For there, too, Christian vision, mission, justice, care, are to be wrought out and lived toward, not simply announced or accomplished through applied knowledges.

Second is her unstated recognition that it is too easy to dismiss some congregational members' longing and anxieties about change as nostalgia or sentimentality. Their hunger is for God, and some methods for discerning God's presence in their very ordinary lives. Not having been educated in seminary or up to the latest in hermeneutical theory or deconstruction, "naively" they "expect" God's Presence. Here dimensions of the author's work intersect with current interest in the relations among pastoral care, pastoral counseling, and spirituality. Her work on reconstructing the Reformed God contributes well to that dialogue.

As I write it is Easter Sunday. Congregations—even with their exhausted clerical leadership—anticipate living into the promises of joy and reconciliation they long for. Few pastoral care texts mention joy as an issue in pastoral care and pastoral practice. Our identification with problems and predicaments may even lead toward moments of despair or cynicism or concerns apparently far removed from the everyday living of the ordinary parishioners. Authors may be driven by concern for academic respectability and even political correctness. But this author takes with full seriousness the rightful expectation that Christian hope has something to do with real joy, real reconciliation, and, indirectly at least, this text leans toward taking that deep hunger with full seriousness. Care may be about crisis, and counseling about despair, and consultation about difficulties. But the careseeker in congregational living has been led to believe that somewhere, even in the midst of shared suffering, there is also shared joy. Indeed, a focus on joy should be at the heart of continuing the very rich dialogue begun here.

Peggy Way

Preface

All persons of faith are called to care for others as an extension of the ministry of Jesus Christ. Feminist perspectives equip those in ministry to shape more equitable pastoral relationships, to assess the multidimensional needs they encounter, and to respond in a manner that more accurately reflects and anticipates God's active presence. This book introduces feminist theology and psychotherapy as sources for caregivers, counselors, and others in ministry who want to draw from current revisions in theology and therapeutic theory. As an introduction, the discussion to follow is a marking point along the way, a "house to live in for a while," as one feminist theologian has suggested, leaving the windows open and the door ajar, as we construct and reconstruct how best to participate in what God is doing.

Feminist influence in pastoral care is both critical and constructive. By opening our eyes to see problems from the diverse experiences of persons in need, enabling us to hear and respond to the larger social and cultural issues evident in an immediate dilemma, and encouraging us to imagine and demonstrate faith in God, who calls forth new creation, feminist revisioning of pastoral care attends to suffering and works toward its alleviation. Through twenty-five years of pastoral ministry, I have listened to careseekers expressing desire to know and be faithful to God, need to resist harm and relieve suffering, and "caughtness" in connections and relations that structured their lives. Making sense of these connections, needs, and desires in dialogue with careseekers, we have often named faithfulness, resistance, or connection as a focus or theme in the caring process. Further, we have wondered together what God is calling forth in a particular situation, how God views the dilemma, or what would change if God drew closer in this time of need. Talk of God's power to re-create and make new, to liberate and free from bondage, or to reconcile, forgive, protect, and gather together has resonated with many persons who want to figure out what to do in light of what God would have them do. The themes of this project in pastoral care are God's actions in creation, liberation, and reconciliation and how we reflect and anticipate what God is doing through faithful response, resistance to harm, and interdependent connections.

My purpose is to discuss selected feminist efforts in theology and therapy and to assess critically the contribution they offer to theory and practice of pastoral care. Feminist revisions do not replace the "homes" that have been constructed along the path of pastoral caring but provide a place to dwell though parts will be torn down, deconstructed, remodeled into something more fitting, or moved on down the road. I invite caregivers to visit this critical perspective emerging from practice of ministry in order to understand human experience as a manifestation of God's extravagant creation and to conceive new creation as increasingly diverse. Caregiving is more effective when we acknowledge our interconnection and interdependence in God's creation, broaden the language and action of faith to include resistance to harm, and use power and potential in caring interpersonal relations to effect larger patterns of need. Feminist influences help pastoral care to reflect and anticipate more fully God's activity and in this way to become more faithful.

Many persons have shared in conversation about the ideas addressed in this book and contributed to its completion. George R. Graham has provided editorial expertise in the process of publication, and his guidance is much appreciated. Two generous mentors, Don Capps and Christie Neuger, provided encouragement and critique several years ago as some of the ideas developed in this text began to take shape. I am grateful to current students and colleagues at Brite Divinity School whose expectations and support call forth teaching ministries and scholarly efforts on behalf of the church.

Twenty-five years ago I was a student in an M.Div. pastoral care class with Professor Peggy Way, who insisted that class members repeat over and over again, "I am a theologian; I am a theologian; I am a theologian." She was persuasive with budding caregivers as we struggled to write our first "working theology" for pastoral ministry. I am among many students whom she invited into the field of pastoral theology and encouraged toward Ph.D. studies, but with the strong recommendation that we first gain much more experience in ministry in the local church. I am so thankful I took her advice.

Chapter One

Theology and the Practice of Ministry

Ray and Janet sat in their living room with the pastor, describing the problems occurring in their family—their fourteen-year-old son's problems at school, a twelve-year-old daughter who seemed to be growing up too fast.[1] When the pastor inquired how they were working together to manage these problems, they acknowledged more arguments than togetherness as parents. In fact, their fifteenth wedding anniversary was the next week, but neither felt like celebrating, and they had made no plans. Janet worked two part-time jobs as a sales clerk to help support the family, and Ray was not getting along with his current employer in a construction job he had held for more than two years. Since the money was good, he was trying to stay on. They confirmed their sense of working as a team to meet their family's financial needs, but little else felt like a joint effort. Janet said that her family lived in the same house but not together, all going their separate ways or sitting silently in front of the television. Describing his lack of energy at the end of each day, Ray said that sitting was about all he could do in the evening. Janet had been praying about this situation for some time but felt no answer had been given.

In another congregation, the pastor visited Clive, a fifty-year-old man who was in the hospital following bypass surgery the previous day. Clive served as a member of the church governing board, and his generous contributions of expertise and money had enabled the church to increase benevolence giving and begin to build an endowment over the past decade. He had divorced and remarried within the past year and had not experienced heart problems in the past, although the pastor was aware that alcohol abuse had been an issue in his first marriage and that Clive had stopped drinking. His father had died in his mid-fifties from heart disease, but Clive was shocked that a routine exam had resulted in surgery. As

---

1. The illustrative material in this project offers composite portrayals drawn from my pastoral work with individuals, families, groups, and congregations in a variety of ministry contexts. I have changed identifying information in order to protect the careseekers' privacy.

an investment broker, he was accustomed to working under high stress, and his doctor had mentioned earlier that day that they would talk more about some lifestyle changes necessary to improve his health. He said to the pastor, "I really don't want to change a thing right now. God knows I'd hate to die when everything is going so well. Maybe this is a wake-up call."

In a third situation of pastoral ministry, the First Community Church of Smithfield had made a concerted effort in the past year to bring in new members. The governing board had followed up on the few visitors who had come to worship, added a Bible study class aimed at young adults, and tried to make the service "friendly" with ample announcements of opportunities for becoming involved. Instead of increasing, however, the membership had continued to decline. The board was discouraged about the repairs needed on the church building and the lack of funds to complete the work. Without new members, the church would not be able to afford a full-time pastor much longer. Many assumed that the current pastor was looking for another position and wondered how they could go on without someone "at the helm" or maintain the outreach efforts they had initiated to low-income families in the immediate neighborhood. One board member voiced her concern: "It seems to me that we've got to change something. I mean—who would join a church that's like a sinking ship, just worried about surviving? Isn't there something else we can do so that people would want to join in, something more than this survival mentality?"

Pastoral care came to play a vital role in each of these situations of ministry. *Pastoral care* is the help and nurture offered in a relationship between a representative of the church and persons seeking care that reflects, as much as possible, the justice and compassion of God. *Pastoral counseling* is a more specific and structured form of care involving an intentional process of identifying problems and discerning and implementing possibilities for change and healing. *Pastoral care consultation* is a process in which an individual equipped through experience and training offers guidance, advice, and/or training to congregations, lay caregivers, or pastors in problem resolution, skill development, or program planning. In all these aspects of ministry—caregiving and its more specific forms of counseling and consultation—pastors and lay caregivers function as theologians who seek to help others. Caregivers make connections between (1) the careseeker and the situation of need and (2) their mutual understanding of who God is and what God may be doing in and through that situation.[2]

---

2. Classic divisions in academic theology locate practical theology as one branch of the theological enterprise along with systematic/philosophical and biblical/historical

Feminist revisions in theology, psychology, and therapy contribute significantly to the accuracy and effectiveness of these connections, and exploring these alternative ways of seeing provides an illuminating, if partial, perspective for pastoral care. Feminist thought emerged from attention to the difference in women and men's experience and analysis of the effects of this difference in social, political, economic, and theological dimensions of life. Valid criticism of overgeneralization about women's experience has highlighted the error of feminist thought that portrays gender alone as an adequate category of analysis when it precludes attention to significant differences among women themselves and fails to link gender with race, age, sexual orientation, and other important categories of human experience. At the same time, feminist perspectives have made it more possible to begin to value difference and diversity, to recognize and resist the destructive force of power as domination, and to encourage effective use of influence and agency among those who have had too little.

For purposes of pastoral care, the critical perspective of feminist thought calls for reconsidering images of God and the consequences of describing relationship with and response to God and for questioning how God's justice and compassion can be more fully reflected in pastoral caring not only with individuals and families but with larger, systemic causes of suffering. Attending to the practical consequences of how caregivers define problems and responsibility for their resolution in dialogue with those who suffer signals the "performative" quality of theology and theory of change in ministry. Feminist theology, therapeutic theory, and political theory are surely not the only sources for pastoral care, but these sources do help caregivers think through their actions, consider theology and theory as "thought experiments" amenable to change, and identify, correct, or reaffirm the congruence between what they believe and what they do in ministry and the consequences of both.

As theologians, caregivers draw from numerous sources, including Scripture and both written and living traditions of faith, making reasoned judgments as they account for the particular situation they are addressing. In addition, persons engaged in pastoral care often use adjunct or supporting disciplines, such as psychology, social theory, or political theory,

---

categories. Practical theology as an academic discipline includes pastoral theology, Christian education, worship and preaching, and administration. Understood in this manner, pastoral theology draws from practice of ministry for critical development of theological understanding.

to understand further and respond to the dimensions of the problem and its context. Drawing from a variety of helping skills, especially empathy and active listening, assessment, and formulation of a problem and its resolution, persons engaged in pastoral ministry bring knowledge and faith commitments as part of their response to need. Theology persistently informs and alters the effective practice of ministry, and if sufficient critical and constructive reflection occurs, theological interpretation itself is changed as a result of its adequacy or inadequacy in understanding and addressing experiences of need.

For caregivers to understand suffering accurately they need to be in dialogue with careseekers, and, on the basis of this shared understanding of the problem, reflect on what faith in and knowledge of God suggests about the problem, its individual, systemic, and cultural dimensions, and what resolution or change is desired and possible. This book is about such moments of reflection and dialogue when people of faith dwell with experiences of sin and suffering, and care and counsel are offered as a reflection and anticipation of God's active presence. Making connections between painful experience and what we know of God is one of a caregiver's most important tasks. Caregivers help to discern how relationships with God and one another are distorted in the current social and cultural context and what is necessary in order to be faithful to God in the midst of this suffering and distortion. Further, adequate theological reflection clarifies the partiality of caring responses, however necessary and appropriate they may be. Although our actions may reflect and anticipate the creativity, liberation, and reconciliation that God provides, our efforts do not necessarily accomplish or inherently lead to them.

Caregivers face numerous challenges as they encounter Ray and Janet, Clive, or the lay leadership at the First Community congregation, and the chapters to follow are extended pastoral theological reflection on these and other situations of pastoral care. Expanding moments for reflection following a pastoral encounter may seem to make things much more complicated than they need to be! Creating problems where none exists is the last thing that most caregivers want, and many would not identify themselves with the academic discipline of pastoral theology. But this is an effort to think through the sources that inform a helpful pastoral response, the relation among those sources, and the consequences of using them, which is the task of pastoral theology.[3] Expanding critical and construc-

---

3. Larry Kent Graham provides a helpful discussion of sources of knowledge in pastoral theology: the practice of a ministry of care, the particular social location and

tive reflection on a few situations of care can enhance pastoral responses in many and may set the stage for further learning as caregivers seek to be faithful to their calling.

Pastoral theologians face several challenges that are addressed in this chapter.[4] First, pastoral theological reflection must be a sufficiently systematic thinking-through or reasoning about a situation of need encountered in ministry, the perspective of a faith tradition, and additional theory from other disciplines to help explain and take action in the situation. Second, systematic reflection in pastoral theology is normally interdisciplinary, using theory from disciplines other than theology in a manner that respects their integrity, avoiding reductionism or syncretism, neither oversimplifying a discipline nor combining assumptions without regard for their difference. Third, the historical assumptions of theology and adjunct theory become evident in this process of reflection, as an emphasis on the past, present, or future is made explicit, suggesting crucial differences in the focus of a pastoral response. Fourth, the special purview of pastoral theology is to be pragmatic, concerned with action, and to evaluate the consequences and effectiveness of theological reflection and practice of ministry.

An additional challenge faced by most caregivers is hearing a careseeker's experience of a problem without assuming too quickly that we understand. Reflecting on situations of need in pastoral care, a pastoral theologian analyzes whether or not the careseeker's understanding of a problem has been accurately heard and privileged, or given a special value, rather than foreclosed by the caregiver's view, or inappropriately overtaken by a theological or theoretical framework. As a result, pastoral theologians must attend to their own personal social location and its effects in their interpretations, limiting the claims they are making. The

---

personhood of the caregiver, a social or cultural/political theory that helps to explain the particular context of care, the religious tradition in both its formal and operational dimensions, and secular disciplines such as theories of personality or psychotherapy. *Care of Persons, Care of Worlds: A Psychosystems Approach to Pastoral Care and Counseling* (Nashville: Abingdon, 1992), 20–21.

4. The issues identified are informed by discussions in Donald Browning, ed., *Practical Theology* (San Francisco: Harper & Row, 1983); Rebecca Chopp, *Saving Work: Feminist Practice of Theological Education* (Louisville: Westminster John Knox, 1991); Lewis S. Mudge and James N. Poling, eds., *Formation and Reflection: The Promise of Practical Theology* (Minneapolis: Fortress Press, 1987); and James N. Poling and Donald E. Miller, *Foundations for a Practical Theology of Ministry* (Nashville: Abingdon, 1985).

social location of those intended to hear and respond to the reflection is also identified, often stated as the church and/or the academy and sometimes as a wider social or cultural "audience" or group of conversation partners.

In subsequent chapters I turn to reflection upon specific situations of pastoral care, analysis of the theology and theory that informed a pastoral response, and offer suggestions for revising pastoral theology and practice. Due to the variety of theologies and therapies identified as "feminist," it is not possible to agree with them all, and in my view that is part of the benefit of exploring this range of perspectives. I argue that feminist thought provides a critical perspective that pushes at the limits of our theological and therapeutic assumptions and provides space for revitalizing our sense of purpose and effectiveness in ministry and clarifying appropriate boundaries and relations among the sources informing our care. In the sections remaining in this chapter, I explore issues currently faced by pastoral theologians without, of course, fully resolving them. My intention is to identify marking points from which pastors and other caregivers, as well as those engaged in the academic discipline of pastoral theology, may choose to assess their own efforts in integrating theory and practice and in reflecting theologically on situations of care.

Challenges in Pastoral Theology

Pastoral caregivers use theological knowledge and demonstrate faith commitments in responding to suffering and need. The intersection of what caregivers know and what those seeking care articulate about their experience and need is the meeting point of *praxis,* the ongoing mutual relation of theory and practice, or theology and situation. Pastoral caregivers bring prior knowledge and experience to the task of assessing need and what can be done to address it. When the pastor visits Ray and Janet, all three have some knowledge of respective faith perspectives based on participation in a local church. Knowledge of family systems and feminist psychotherapies may aid a pastor in hearing the roles and responsibilities Ray and Janet are taking in their family. The pastor may also invite them to say a little more about their sense of what sustains family members' commitments to one another and what rituals or routines they have tried that have made intimacy more possible. A caregiver may also wonder with them about the culture-bound, gender-based expectations reflected in their situation and how they fit or don't fit with a sense of what God is calling forth in their family.

As the pastor listens to Clive describe his health crisis and how it is interfering with all that is going well in his life, he offers empathy and encourages Clive to express his thoughts and feelings. The pastor may invite Clive to reflect on the meaning and value of his health and affirm the strength and courage he has demonstrated in choosing to care for himself in the past. At some point after the immediate crisis has passed, the pastor may recall with Clive his statement about God's knowing he doesn't want to die now and ask Clive how this brush with mortality has changed him, his sense of purpose or place in the larger scheme of things.

The leaders of the First Community congregation are wondering how they will manage the mission and ministry of their congregation if the pastor leaves and want to do more than just survive as a community of faith. By default or by choice, they may take on more responsibility for pastoral care in the congregation and local community and find ways to equip themselves for meaningful and effective ministries of care for persons in need. A pastor or pastoral consultant may work with the lay leadership, encouraging them to strengthen the ecumenical connections with other congregations in their local community. Perhaps an alternative to the image of "sinking ship" would emerge so that they could participate in partnership with several congregations and discover the unique and vital role to which they are called in a collaborative expression of care.

The theological perspective of this project in revisioning locates its roots in the Reformed tradition, with its emphasis on certain theological themes, creeds, confessions, and practices of faith. Central theological affirmations in this tradition as interpreted by my own denomination are the sovereignty of God and the rediscovery of God's grace in Jesus Christ as revealed in the Scriptures.[5] In identifying my theological "location," I disclose the particularity of sources that influence this project in order that others may recognize differences with their own, equally valid, tradition or theological location. Reflecting and anticipating God's activity mark an important theological distinction and relation between our purpose and action in pastoral ministry and what we know of God's purpose in redemptive acts of liberation and reconciliation. Throughout this project, I commend pastoral ministry as "anticipatory activity," by which I mean human action in response to need that also moves toward a new future.[6] Claiming that we reflect and anticipate God's action

5. Other themes of the Reformed tradition are stated in *The Constitution of the Presbyterian Church (U.S.A.)*, part 2, *Book of Order* (Louisville: Office of the General Assembly, Presbyterian Church (U.S.A.), 1999–2000), G-2.0500.

6. The notion of "anticipatory activity" is informed by Rebecca Chopp's discus-

through our own does not mean that we bring about the coming "kingdom" or that we are embarked on an inevitable progression toward the new creation. In partnership with those in need, caregivers seek to discern in present dilemmas what may be partial but nonetheless faithful reflection and anticipation of God's presence and activity. We know of God's action through Scripture, the witness of the faith community through time, and the prompting of the Spirit, as we are able to understand them in our personal and communal experience.

A number of practices of faith, or active forms of life together, appear consistently in the Reformed tradition.[7] Though the practices do not cause faith, they do "put us in a position where we may recognize and participate in the work of God's grace in the world." The list is summarized as follows, quoting in full the last two practices:

worshiping God together;

telling the Christian story to one another;

interpreting together the Scriptures and the history of the church's experience;

praying together and by ourselves;

confessing our sin to one another;

tolerating one another's failures and encouraging one another in the work each must do;

carrying out specific faithful acts of service and witness;

suffering with and for each other and all whom Jesus showed us to be our neighbors;

providing hospitality and care;

sion in *The Praxis of Suffering: An Interpretation of Liberation and Political Theologies* (Maryknoll, N.Y.: Orbis Books, 1986), 118–33. Based on her analysis of the theologies of Gustavo Gutiérrez, Johann Baptist Metz, and Jürgen Moltmann, Chopp discusses the anthropology of praxis in liberation theology in three categories: the political nature, the intersubjective character, and the anticipatory freedom of human existence. I argue that liberation theology and feminist theology, which builds on it, point out the political nature of the sin of oppression and the intersubjective structuring of this distortion of power. Drawing upon Chopp's analysis, I use the term "anticipatory" in relation to human freedom and action, but acknowledge our limits and partiality as distinguished from God's freedom and action.

7. Theology and Worship Ministry Unit, Presbyterian Church (U.S.A.), *Growing in the Life of Christian Faith* (Louisville: Presbyterian Church (U.S.A.) Distribution Management Services, 1989).

listening and talking attentively to one another about our particular experiences in life;

struggling together to become conscious of and understand the nature of the context in which we live;

criticizing and resisting all those powers and patterns (both within the church and in the world as a whole) that destroy human beings, corrode human community, and injure God's creation;

working together to maintain and create social structures and institutions which will sustain life in the world in ways that accord with God's will.[8]

Through various ministries, including ministries of care and counseling, the community of faith fosters and sustains these practices of faith. Every form of ministry is responsible for doing its part to establish and sustain all the practices. In other words, a ministry such as pastoral care may be evaluated by the degree to which all of the practices are involved in and sustained by this form of ministry. I have found such denominational resources to be quite helpful in assessing the practice of ministry in the local congregation and in my current function as a seminary faculty member, teaching pastoral theology and providing pastoral counseling.

At the same time, such guidance is helpful in a context that affords some freedom of interpretation and grants authority to draw from numerous sources to inform both theology and practice. In order to respond more adequately to suffering and to participate in healing among persons in need, I have found feminist perspectives in theology, therapy, and political theory particularly helpful.[9] Without some critical perspective, our assumptions are less explicit and open to evaluation, and we are less likely to hear and clarify our understanding of the particular experience of others, to acknowledge the limits of what we offer, and to learn from careseekers what faithfulness looks like in their situation. What appear to be personal or individual problems are so often caused or exacerbated by larger social and cultural forces, systemic forms of sin such as sexism, racism, classism, heterosexism, and violence. Feminist thought provides one means to reflect critically and constructively on power arrangements in interpersonal relationships, structures, and institutions.[10]

---

8. Ibid., 27–28.

9. Sheila Ruth suggests that feminism may be a perspective, a worldview, a political theory, a spiritual focus, or a kind of activism but that there are certain beliefs, values, and attitudes that are held in common among feminists. *Issues in Feminism: A First Course in Women's Studies* (Boston: Houghton Mifflin, 1980), 4–5, 396.

10. Gerda Lerner defines patriarchy in this way: "It implies that men hold power

Among feminist theologians, I have resonated most closely with the works of Letty Russell because of her methodological balance in utilizing the Christian tradition and women's experience as sources for theology.[11] I have found her work to be a good "fit" with my own formation in faith because she has used women's experience as an authoritative source for theology without making it the only criterion for theological revision. As Russell interprets our hope in God's future, she emphasizes the advent of God's future coming toward us as a promise:

> How can we live now as if the horizon of that future has already broken into our lives through the Spirit of Jesus Christ? The discovery of this new horizon of freedom leads us to actions because God hopes for us, and it is up to us to live now as if the "form of this world is passing away" and the new creation is already present in our lives.[12]

Russell's work on partnership in the new creation points toward a fuller sense of our interdependence, but it does not adequately address the differences or conflicts involved in partnership or take into account the dynamics within an individual that contribute to or disrupt these purposeful relationships. Some criticize Russell's thought for its neoorthodox doctrinal perspective that recognizes a "canon within the canon," that is, that views God's redemptive and liberating activity in Jesus Christ as the essence of biblical tradition. Elisabeth Schüssler Fiorenza critiques Russell's approach for failing to analyze the function of Scripture in oppressing women and the poor.[13]

---

in all the important institutions of society and that women are deprived of access to such power. It does not imply that women are either totally powerless or totally deprived of rights, influences, and resources." Gerda Lerner, *The Creation of Patriarchy* (Oxford: Oxford University Press, 1986), app., 239.

11. I refer particularly to several works by Letty Russell: *Human Liberation in a Feminist Perspective: A Theology* (1974), *The Future of Partnership* (1979), *Growth in Partnership* (1981), *Becoming Human* (1982), *Household of Freedom: Authority in Feminist Theology* (1987), and *Church in the Round: A Feminist Interpretation of the Church* (1993). These books were published by Westminster Press of Philadelphia, except the last one, which was published by Westminster John Knox of Louisville.

12. Russell, *Human Liberation,* 42. Russell states that feminist theology is by definition liberation theology because it is concerned with the liberation of all people to become full participants in society. She understands liberation theology as "an attempt to reflect upon the experience of oppression and our actions for the new creation of a more humane society." Ibid., 20.

13. Elisabeth Schüssler Fiorenza, *In Memory of Her: A Feminist Theological Reconstruction of Christian Origins* (New York: Crossroad, 1983), 14–16.

In recent years, I have drawn upon feminist theological perspectives that challenge Russell's liberal orientation toward what some call a "utopian future" and insist upon more evidence of justice in the present.[14] Although I have shared Russell's liberal theological viewpoint, I do not claim that we are in partnership with God, although I view our relationship with one another this way. I use feminist theologies that promote self-critical awareness among those seeking freedom or power, recognizing the contradictory motives and desires that may fuel our efforts on behalf of liberation. From my perspective, pastoral care and counseling are informed by, and instructive for, feminist theology and the Reformed tradition. Through their ministry caregivers are able to identify a more adequate theory of self or theological anthropology and a vision of the "good" in which freedom and power are used in anticipation of the reconciliation of all creation. Numerous recent works by pastoral theologians informed by feminist perspectives offer resources for reflection on and enhancement of caring ministries.[15]

Theological themes have emerged in my pastoral encounters with persons in need, and three of these themes—faithful response to God, resistance to harm, and connections with one another—are explored here. In identifying these themes, I have tried to privilege the voice of the per-

14. In this project, I am in dialogue primarily with the work of Rita Nakashima Brock, Rebecca Chopp, Sallie McFague, and Letty Russell.

15. Examples of literature in feminist pastoral theology include Denise M. Ackerman and Riet Bons-Storm, eds., *Liberating Faith Practices: Feminist Practical Theologies in Context* (Louvain, Belgium: Peeters, 1998); Riet Bons-Storm, *The Incredible Woman: Listening to Women's Silence in Pastoral Care and Counseling* (Nashville: Abingdon, 1997); Pamela D. Couture, *Blessed Are the Poor? Women's Poverty, Family Policy, and Practical Theology* (Nashville: Abingdon, 1991); Valerie DeMarinis, *Critical Caring: A Feminist Model for Pastoral Psychology* (Louisville: Westminster John Knox, 1993); Carrie Doehring, *Taking Care: Monitoring Power Dynamics and Relational Boundaries in Pastoral Care and Counseling* (Nashville: Abingdon, 1995); Elaine Graham, *Transforming Practice: Pastoral Theology in an Age of Uncertainty* (London: Mowbray, 1996); Bonnie Miller-McLemore and Brita Gill-Austern, eds., *Feminist and Womanist Pastoral Theology* (Nashville: Abingdon, 1999); Jeanne Stevenson Moessner, ed., *Through the Eyes of Women: Insights for Pastoral Care* (Minneapolis: Fortress Press, 1996); Christie Cozad Neuger, *Counseling Women: A Narrative Pastoral Approach* (Nashville: Abingdon, 2001); Christie Cozad Neuger, ed., *The Arts of Ministry: Feminist-Womanist Approaches* (Louisville: Westminster John Knox, 1996); Christie Cozad Neuger and James N. Poling, *The Care of Men* (Nashville: Abingdon, 1997); and Carol Saussy, *God Images and Self-Esteem: Empowering Women in Patriarchal Society* (Louisville: Westminster John Knox, 1991).

son seeking care, allowing a problem and its resolution to be shaped in the terms articulated by the careseeker. Faithful response, resistance, and connection are dynamic, relational terms that point to the need for continuity and change over time and place in one's sense of self in response to God, appropriate resistance to harm resulting from both personal and systemic sin, and the need for healthy, interdependent connections with others. Individual and communal faithfulness involves persistence in making sense of identity and purpose in relation to God. Resistance may effect changes in the causes and conditions of suffering resulting from misuse of freedom and power. Connection, in its desirable forms, affirms the interdependence of individuals and a healthy, hopeful way to live in family, social, and ecological systems.

The purpose of identifying these relational themes as theological is to locate explicitly the care situation in the redemptive presence and activity of God.[16] Assumptions about theology are operative in most pastoral ministry, and rendering assumptions explicit allows critical reflection on the caregiver and careseeker's views of the situation in relation to God. Historically, pastoral care has often drawn from doctrinal theology in order to reflect on particular needs, and for many pastors that continues to be an effective means of "doing" theology. Rather than "applying" a theological position or viewpoint, I intend to open space for reflection so that assumptions about God's nature as Creator, incarnate Son, and living Spirit, about suffering and healing, sin and salvation, are subject to critique and revision.

Pastoral Response to Particular Need

Pastoral care continues to be shaped by the theological concerns of the specific faith tradition in which it occurs, but a new focus on the "expertise" of those who seek care and the context in which their needs have emerged has altered our task as caregivers. In fact, careseekers are now more accurately understood as participants in the process of care,

---

16. Larry Graham has discussed a growing separation between theological academic preparation and clinical practice. He has identified critical theological norms that pastoral theology offers pastoral counseling: fuller realization of the image of God in a concrete situation, liberation from bondage as relational justice, and hope in the face of despair. Although I do not identify the themes of this project as "norms" per se, my purpose is similar in bridging theology and practice. See Larry Kent Graham, "From Impasse to Innovation in Pastoral Theology and Counseling," *Journal of Pastoral Theology* 6 (summer 1996): 17–35.

influencing the definition of the problems they face, identifying a means to the resolution of their difficulties, and exercising agency in implementing this means. A significant shift has occurred in the relationship between caregivers and careseekers toward more equitable relations, valuing of difference, and fuller regard for the resources people in need bring to a process of change. Pastoral care can no longer be understood as one-way "giving" by an expert to a recipient and is better understood as a cooperative or collaborative effort in which a representative of a faith tradition plays a significant, but not dominant, role in the process. The ability to "locate" or position oneself appropriately as caregiver, using authority or power as a caring participant in change, is a crucial component in contemporary pastoral care.

One early experience challenged my theological view and capacity to offer care in an ecumenical urban ministry working with single-parent families and the young women who headed these families. A second pastoral experience was in a suburban church that hosted an office for the local women's shelter and my occasional leadership of a support group for women who had used the shelter's resources. As I listened to the stories of women in these contexts and began to hear their day-to-day struggle, the inadequacy of my liberal theology and therapeutic knowledge as theories to explain and help address their problems became quite obvious. I had read some feminist literature and feminist theology, had addressed issues of inclusive language in seminary, and as a single woman, faced some obstacles in finding a ministry position. But my white, middle-class feminism, with its assumptions of privilege and possibility, was insufficient for understanding or altering the circumstances of the women and families in these early pastoral experiences.

The women who participated in the urban ministry program were young. Most were white, some were black or Hispanic, and many received public assistance. Nearly all had experienced verbal and physical abuse from parents and/or ex-husbands or boyfriends. In the peer groups we developed, the women heard and learned from one another, often through stories with worldly-wise humor about how to work the systems with which their lives were intertwined—which counselor to ask for at the vocational rehabilitation center, how to appease the principal when their children had problems at school, what doctor would listen to their health concerns before writing the prescription, how to prepare for the Graduate Equivalency Diploma, what women's clothing had just arrived at the church clothing bank, where diapers were on sale that week. Many, many of the stories were not humorous, especially those describing their attempts to protect themselves from abusive ex-husbands or boyfriends. Violence and misuse of power became a pattern for a few of the women themselves, and we held workshops on parenting skills and used personnel from Child Protective Services as a resource.

The women talked with one another about their experiences in the church and their sense of relationship with God. A few of the women attended the local congregations that sponsored the ministry; some attended Pentecostal revivals occasionally; most had clear notions of God as all-powerful and judgmental and believed that their difficulties in life were just punishment for the things they had done wrong. They believed that if they tried hard enough and behaved well enough, God would reward them with a better, safer life. It was difficult for me to empathize with some of the suffering the women experienced because it frightened and frustrated me. I had learned to interpret suffering in very individual terms, to identify the ways in which we contribute to our own suffering, with self-reliance as a primary healing antidote.

Something about the interwoven, recursive nature of the problems the women faced exposed the inadequacy of the theological and psychological theories with which I was equipped as a pastoral caregiver. An individual, existential, or family systems approach in pastoral care did not sufficiently explain the web of power relationships and interdependencies that characterized their lives. At the same time, the women themselves reinforced the value of self-reliance in the stories they shared as a group and encouraged one another in realistic individual initiatives that would improve their respective situations. In this way, the group functioned as a community that valued and attended to individuals in their particularity and helped them to overcome the sense of isolation from which many of the women suffered. Group participation did not circumvent self-reliance but rather enhanced and strengthened it through experiences of mutuality, criticism, and support. We began conversations with the local women's shelter and police department to try to decrease the response time for "domestic disputes." We participated in lobbying the state legislature to make it easier to obtain a restraining order against someone who had been violent in the past. We developed one-to-one partnerships between women in the local sponsoring churches and the women in the program for purposes of support and crisis intervention, within specified limits.

A second focus in my ministry of care with women and men has occurred over many years in different congregations and ministry contexts where I served as pastor and pastoral counselor. In each situation the person was practicing faith in a congregation or articulating a faith perspective in relation to the problem he or she was currently facing, and the person's desire to be faithful was not in question. Some of these careseekers had studied Scripture individually and in groups for many years and were struggling with how to be faithful to God, to themselves, and to their families. They acknowledged experiencing harm in their family roles, both chosen and imposed, and in the process of care or counseling, we probed some of the assumptions about those roles. Their faith perspectives were forms of connection, of staying with the potential and hope for resolution of difficulties as we discussed possibilities for healthier relationships and constructive action, of which they were capable. Their practice of faith in the face of problems also took the form of resistance to further erosion of emotional vitality and, in a positive sense, self-protection, as they stayed in a family or work situation until a problem could be more fully resolved. These practices were more like resistance as endurance, withstanding a force that opposed health or well-being, until change became possible.

A sustaining type of pastoral care response reflected an understanding of God as Creator, affirmed the inestimable value of the person created in God's image, and the courage it often took to claim this self-understanding in the midst of a harmful situation. We began to speak of this form of resistance as opposing harm for the sake of more just connections with others and elaborated on appropriate forms of resistance and connection on the basis of faith in God. Reflection on these experiences of pastoral response to need has challenged the theological perspective I hold as a Reformed and feminist pastoral theologian and altered the theories from supporting disciplines that I have used to inform pastoral care. A praxis orientation in pastoral care and counseling privileges or values the careseeker's knowledge and experience, definition of the problem, and identification of its resolution and draws upon the knowledge and experience of the caregiver to the extent that it is accurate and effective in addressing that particular situation.

As will become evident, the caregiver does not usually need to introduce a theological perspective or interpretation but functions to highlight or call forth prior understanding of the problem expressed by careseekers as it corresponds to or contradicts a sense of God's presence and activity. Rather than viewing pastoral care and counseling as application of certain theological principles or therapeutic skills, I understand *praxis* as an ongoing process wherein knowledge leads from practice toward theory toward practice in an ongoing, spiral pattern. Responding to particular situations of suffering exposes the limitations of both theology and theory from supporting disciplines (often psychotherapy, social, or political theory). The caregiver, as pastoral theologian, continues the corrective praxis spiral with critical reflection and alters her response to suffering, correcting the theology and theory that informed the response. This project is an extended moment in that process, a moment of critical and constructive reflection on theology and theory in the midst of ongoing praxis.

One of the criticisms of an orientation toward praxis is that it lapses into a relativism that prevents generalization beyond a particular situation or experience. In his discussion of praxis, Richard Bernstein suggests there is a way through the hazard of relativism when utilizing such an orientation.[17] He states that the issue of objectivism and relativism is not a theoretical problem, but a practical task. Bernstein says that we desperately need to seize upon those experiences and struggles in which there are still "glimmerings of solidarity and the promise of dialogical communities in which there can be genuine mutual participation."[18] Bernstein describes our contemporary situation as paradoxical in that "power creates counterpower (resistance) and reveals the vulnerability of power" when forces that seem beyond our control and appear to undermine and inhibit communal life inadvertently "create new and frequently unpredictable forms of solidarity."[19]

For purposes of pastoral care and counseling, I interpret Bernstein's statement to mean that focusing on experiences in which solidarity and community are possible does not end in relativism. Attention to the particular, a focus in pastoral ministry, may create new connections and forms of community beyond the specific or individual situation. Rather than making generalizations on behalf of others, attending to and interpreting a specific situation as it is understood by those in it may indeed lead to relationship, insight, and communal action that otherwise might not have occurred. Oriented toward the careseeker's view of the situation, the caregiver does not impose an interpretation but, as a participant invited to do so, takes responsibility for collaborative discernment with the careseeker, discerning the meaning and implications of faith in God. In this manner, theology persistently informs and alters the practice of ministry,

---

17. Richard J. Bernstein, *Beyond Objectivism and Relativism* (Philadelphia: University of Pennsylvania Press, 1988).

18. Ibid., 228.

19. Ibid.

and theological interpretation is itself changed as a result of its adequacy or inadequacy in understanding and addressing experiences of need.

A feminist perspective enhances pastoral ministry because it provides a critical view of the effects of power misused as dominance or unclaimed, and it offers a means for interpreting and changing individuals and the systems and structures that affect us. At the same time, I acknowledge criticism about the relativism of a praxis orientation in terms of the limits of a feminist or liberation theology perspective. Privileging emancipation over faith tradition, as Rebecca Chopp recommends, represents a limited view of a biblical and theological tradition that includes themes of freedom and liberation. Problems encountered in pastoral care and counseling are not always those of emancipation or liberation and not often *only* a question of enhancing human freedom, even for those who are suffering. Other considerations have to do with health, in the holistic sense of spiritual, physical, and psychological well-being of individuals, families, and communities, and the "health" of other systems and the environment itself. Some choices on behalf of health and well-being may limit freedom. Further, a fully Christian theological view understands health and well-being as anticipatory of God's fulfillment of redemption when both liberation and reconciliation will be fully realized for humanity and creation. Though a rhetoric of oppression is an effective strategy for change in locating the structural causes of suffering, it may also obscure the ambiguity of sin and harm, and discernment of this ambiguity is a necessary component of effective pastoral ministry.

In addition, rhetoric about oppression may inadvertently render persons less able to change themselves or the causes of their suffering if the individual or oppressed group is understood primarily in the defining experience of oppression. This project seeks to recognize and respond to the interdependence of individuals and the larger social systems in which we live and to affirm human freedom and capacity for creative, transformative activity. It is within interdependent relations that human capacities for creative resistance and empathic connection are expressed, anticipating the liberation and reconciliation that God brings to fulfillment. Understanding God's presence and action in terms of liberation is necessary but not sufficient, and the additional themes of re-creation and reconciliation, though still partial, offer a fuller theology of God for purposes of pastoral care and counseling.[20] This emphasis on the relation and distinction be-

---

20. A similar point is made in Daniel L. Migliore, *Called to Freedom: Liberation Theology and the Future of Christian Doctrine* (Philadelphia: Westminster Press, 1980).

tween what we do and what God does is one way of affirming human agency on behalf of change *and* claiming faith in the living God who may choose to work in and through us, but whose purpose and action we do not fully comprehend or embody. Pastoral theologians working from a liberal, reformist perspective (myself included) may ignore certain aspects of experience in order to perceive a unity that does not exist, as Chopp has suggested in her critique of the "liberal project" of Christianity.[21] Because all experience is interpreted experience, Chopp's criticism offers a thread of suspicion about any attempt to fit experience into a theory or theological view, whether liberal and revisionist or radical and revolutionary.

Feminist Theology and Psychotherapy

In the chapters to follow, I draw from feminist theology and theories of self and psychotherapy as sources of knowledge in pastoral theological reflection and as theories of change in practice of ministry. A brief overview of these sources of knowledge for pastoral theological reflection signals the range and limits of this effort and a rationale for the selection of these sources. The variety of efforts for change embraced by the term "feminist" calls for careful identification of the criteria for interpreting a situation of pastoral care or a problem presented in pastoral counseling. Naming these sources as "feminist" locates them in a historical movement and an evolving ideology. The women's movement traces a variety of efforts for political change beginning in the nineteenth century. Some efforts associated with liberal, moderate means of political change have emphasized equal opportunity and individual political and economic rights.[22]

Socialist efforts for political change have demanded actual equality and take more into account the effects of class differences. The socialist stream within feminism locates the need for change in larger economic structures

---

21. Chopp states that understanding is an inadequate goal for theological reflection and that the need for transformation and change must direct methodology. She views the liberal project of Christianity as "a project that engineers a basic identity between two abstract referents for interpretation—human experience and Christian tradition—and that expresses this unity as the meaningfulness and truth of authentic existence, masking the compliancy of Christianity with what Johann Baptist Metz calls bourgeois existence." Rebecca Chopp, "Practical Theology and Liberation," in *Formation and Reflection,* ed. Mudge and Poling, 121.

22. Ruth, *Issues in Feminism,* 4–5.

and social systems of society. Radical feminism, another stream within the women's movement, analyzes patriarchal values in the culture that prescribe certain roles for women, particularly within the family. But common elements exist even amidst the variety of feminist streams of thought and activity. One among these elements is perhaps the most common: that women are valued in and of themselves and not through the distorted "masculism" that mistakes male perspectives and attitudes for all human perceptions.

Feminist theology helps us discern how our relationships with God and one another are distorted, in part, by patriarchy and decide what action is necessary in order for us to be faithful to God in the midst of this suffering and distortion. Selected feminist theologians (Rita Nakashima Brock, Sallie McFague, and Sharon D. Welch) raise significant questions that contribute to this effort in revisioning theology on the basis of practice of ministry.[23] I have earlier described resonance with Russell's perspective and the congruence of her innovation within the Reformed tradition. I have found Russell's focus on new creation to be quite informative in care situations when a distinction between personal responsibility for change and God's larger part in re-creation is needed. McFague's theology of personal metaphors for God (mother, lover, and friend) and the metaphor of the world as God's body are imaginative invitations to reconsider how we think of and relate to God. Her revision of the relation of God and the world through alternative models and her notion of "recentering" in relation to the body of God (creation) offer constructive alternatives for pastoral care.

While I do not share the "qualified nihilism" evident in some of Welch's thought, her efforts to acknowledge the relative value of claims to truth and the normative value of communicative ethics in feminist liberation theology warrant exploration. Welch's theology defines the term "resistance" as challenge to structural evil, particular forms of oppression, and particular configurations of power and knowledge. In company with many other liberation theologians, Welch insists that the criterion of truth for liberation theology is practice, the actual process of liberation as it occurs in particular situations in history. She suggests that theologians pay

---

23. Rita Nakashima Brock, *Journeys by Heart: A Christology of Erotic Power* (New York: Crossroad, 1988); Sallie McFague, *The Body of God: An Ecological Theology* (Minneapolis: Fortress Press, 1993); and *Models of God: Theology for an Ecological, Nuclear Age* (Philadelphia: Fortress Press, 1987); Sharon D. Welch, *Communities of Resistance and Solidarity: A Feminist Theology of Liberation* (Maryknoll, N.Y.: Orbis Books, 1985).

attention to what makes it possible for people to resist oppressive institutions. Welch focuses on the "communal matrix" of responsible action in which oppressed persons engage in long-term struggle and persistent action toward fundamental social change.

Use of the word "resistance" in political movements to describe action for change in the status quo is ironic given its traditional use in psychotherapy for avoidance of needed change. In some practices of therapy, if a client is apparently resisting change on behalf of a healthier self, thwarting goals she herself has identified, the therapist may try to use the resistance on behalf of the desired change. The client can then move on to fewer, or at least "healthier," defenses. In addition to this understanding of resistance as intrapsychic event, this project explores a political definition of resistance as it connotes challenging evil or oppression. Similarities and differences between these two understandings of resistance will assess whether political and psychological notions of resistance are more compatible than they may at first appear.

Brock offers an interpretation of the healing and empowering that can occur in experiences of Christian community. For purposes of this discussion, the focus is primarily on her notion of an empowered community resulting from Jesus' presence. Brock insists that the demystifying of power as dominance and subordination must be accompanied by a move toward self-critical awareness and self-affirmation. She points to the necessity of relationships in community that support and develop the "play space" to demystify destructive powers not only in social systems and other individuals but in ourselves as well. The presence and work of life-giving power, the "truly christological" as she states it, is in the empowering connections people experience in community that witness to both brokenness and sacredness in people's lives. A critique of Brock's Christology can be made from the perspective of some womanist and Latina liberation theologians for whom relationship with the individual person Jesus remains predominant in any christological formulation. I will take this critical perspective into account in affirmation of the plurality that exists among feminist theological perspectives.

Brock's reformulation of Christology appears to diminish understandings of the individual, historical Jesus in an effort to emphasize the influence of his community and the ways in which the community "co-created" him. In my view, we cannot "lose the individual" in an attempt to focus on community, and there is a better way to highlight the mutual influence of community and individual. I argue that "heart to heart" relationships in the community Brock describes may be better understood as interdependent connections and that these relationships anticipate the liberation and reconciliation made possible in Jesus Christ. Further, I suggest that a feminist theological understanding of the Christ of faith requires attention to reconstructions of the historical Jesus in order that our efforts on behalf of liberation and reconciliation continue to undergo ideological relativization. Brock's work provides ample ground for exploring issues of self or individual in community from a theological perspective.

McFague, Welch, and Brock are theological sources for pastoral theology that shape interpretations of experience and the actions that can change situations of need. I use these sources, not because they offer complete theological perspectives or because all "fit" well with the Reformed theological tradition, but because they speak to key issues that arise in pastoral care and counseling informed by feminist views. Pragmatic attention to present action and the consequences of theological formulations offers some qualification of Russell's optimistic search for small signs of the new creation. A more balanced affirmation of the transcendent, liberative power of God, as well as Welch's emphasis on God's immanence, makes it more possible for persons to persist in efforts for justice and healing. In addition, the spirit Christology that Brock commends, focusing on the community inspired by Christ, is an important contribution but cannot replace relationship with the person Jesus Christ or the inspiration and correction this relationship offers.

The feminist models of psychotherapy and theory of self I discuss in chapter 3 also reflect diversity within feminist thought. Theories of psychology or psychotherapy that focus only on gender difference and complementarity or on women's oppression and victimization are necessary but not adequate for purposes of care and counseling. No single theory of psychotherapy or self is complete enough to render a sufficiently complex picture of the individual self and the self in relationship with other individuals and systems. But negotiating the hazards of feminist theory is possible if notions of complementarity of the sexes do not perpetuate sex-role stereotyping or biological determinism. It is possible to focus on oppression and harm in patriarchal society without losing sight of human capacities for resilient action and agency.

A *theory of self,* or personality, is a description of how a person's thoughts, feelings, and behavior are organized within an identified intrapsychic structure, based upon observation and self-report. Such theory includes explicit or implicit assumptions regarding health and human nature and regarding the relationships between individuals, their families, and the larger systems with which their lives are interconnected. A *theory of psychotherapy* is a description of the process by which a person moves toward greater health or resolution of pain and suffering through relationship with a therapist or counselor, based on a particular theory of personality.

Feminist psychotherapies developed by Laura S. Brown and by Mary Ballou and Nancy W. Gabalac and a theory of the development of the self from the work of Carol Gilligan and her colleagues are sources for pastoral care and counseling from a supporting discipline.[24] In addition to exploring these psychotherapies, I will make brief reference to the work in self psychology of Heinz Kohut for a focus on the coherence and internal consistency of the self.[25] The theories are not intended to present fully the breadth of feminist psychotherapy or psychology, but they do offer a more complex mix for the purposes of pastoral theological revision. The feminist theories speak almost exclusively of women's experience, and I intend to respect the integrity of this choice. At the same time, I extend the implications of these models to experiences of men as well as women to the extent that interpreting resistance to dominance and affirmation of relationality are appropriate regardless of gender.

Employing a social-constructionist analysis, many feminist theories of psychotherapy locate the problem addressed through therapy in the political and social context in which the individual experiences it.[26] Brown's theory of psychotherapy views individual problems and need for change as functions of patriarchal dominance. These problems exist not only in

---

24. Mary Ballou and Nancy W. Gabalac, *A Feminist Position on Mental Health* (Springfield, Ill.: Charles C. Thomas, 1985); Laura S. Brown, *Subversive Dialogues: Theory in Feminist Therapy* (New York: Basic Books, 1994); Carol Gilligan, *In a Different Voice: Psychological Theory and Women's Development* (Cambridge: Harvard University Press, 1982); Carol Gilligan, Nona P. Lyons, and Trudy J. Hanmer, *Making Connections: The Relational Worlds of Adolescent Girls at Emma Willard School* (Cambridge: Harvard University Press, 1989); and Carol Gilligan, Annie G. Rogers, and Deborah L. Tolman, eds., *Women, Girls, and Psychotherapy: Reframing Resistance* (New York: Haworth, 1991).

25. Heinz Kohut, *The Restoration of the Self* (Madison, Conn.: International Universities Press, 1977); and *How Does Analysis Cure?* (Chicago: University of Chicago Press, 1984).

26. For discussions of social-construction theory, see works by Kenneth J. Gergen, *The Saturated Self: Dilemmas of Identity in Contemporary Life* (New York: Basic Books); *Realities and Relationship: Soundings in Social Construction* (Cambridge: Harvard University Press, 1994); and *An Invitation to Social Construction* (Thousand Oaks, Calif.: Sage, 2000).

the context but as structures of power that have been internalized and are personified in the lives of clients and therapists as well as in the broader community. The therapy that she commends concerns not only individual suffering but also the social and political meanings of that suffering and the development of a feminist consciousness that moves toward action. Brown explores the paradox of therapists who are functioning as part of "mainstream culture" at the same time as they are developing strategies of resistance to that culture in its overt and subtle structuring of power, or what she calls strategies of "anti-domination."

The feminist model for psychotherapy with women formulated by Ballou and Gabalac identifies two phases of therapy: corrective action and health maintenance. From this viewpoint, patriarchal culture is damaging to women, and their harmful adaptation to that culture causes women to turn to the mental health system for help. The first phase of the therapeutic process includes (1) separation from oppressive systems and structures of power and (2) development of an alternative, positive concept of self. In this phase a woman learns to recognize her own needs and goals and to validate thoughts and feelings that are incongruent with those of the power systems in which she lives. The health-maintenance phase includes experiences of collaboration and community building with other women for the purpose of strategizing to change those systems that have devalued women. Experiences of identification and cooperation with a diverse group of women enable an alliance in which they can work for change in existing systems or create alternatives. I will assess the vision and values in this two-phase psychotherapeutic process in relation to the experiences interpreted in feminist theology as resistance and community. The Ballou and Gabalac model, though insufficient by itself, offers a much needed addition and corrective to theories of psychotherapy that persist in holding individuals responsible for their suffering without attention to contextual factors.

A theory of self developed in collaboration by Carol Gilligan and her colleagues explores the profound influence of connection and relationship in shaping the self. Though this theory claims self is based on relationship rather than separation, I will argue that, as in like Erik Erikson's theory of development, self is shaped in relationship through a process of differentiation.[27] I use Gilligan's theory of self in order to

---

27. Gilligan's theory misconstrues the work of Erik Erikson by suggesting that his theory of human development is based primarily on separation from relationship with significant others. A more careful reading of Erikson's work reveals that his

focus on resistance to disconnection as the particular challenge in the development of self in adolescent girls. This theory of self helps to identify a fuller psychological understanding of certain forms of resistance and connection that may anticipate liberation and reconciliation.

While these feminist theories contribute much to an understanding of the self, they do not adequately portray a sense of the inner self that is more stable or constant over time and perhaps less subject to the changing vicissitudes of environment and social influence. Though feminist perspectives offer a needed corrective by analyzing the social and cultural context in which the self is formed and develops, I utilize the additional perspective of Kohut in order to suggest a fuller theory of self. I argue that this more complete understanding of the human self is necessary for a sufficient sense of the self's freedom and capacity for initiative. The feminist theories of psychotherapy, Gilligan's theory of self-development, and Kohut's self psychology are different in their emphases about how an individual is shaped and influenced and what jeopardizes mental health. They represent perspectives within a broad range of theories of psychology and psychotherapy, and awareness of each enhances the function of this supporting discipline as it informs pastoral care and counseling. Theological understanding of the freedom and embeddedness of the self will be used to clarify what forms of faithfulness, resistance, and connection are desirable for the purpose of pastoral ministry.

Social Location and Hermeneutics

One source of knowledge for the task of pastoral theology is the social location of the caregiver, counselor, or theologian. The question of whether one is attempting critical work from within a tradition or movement or from the perspective of a different tradition, separate from the one being criticized, is especially important in feminist theology. I have worked from a liberal, revisionist perspective within the institutional church, with modest efforts in affirmative action, inclusive language, and addressing issues of sexual harassment and misconduct, all in contexts of more general pastoral ministry. I understand this and other writing

---

discussion of the young child's developmental challenge of autonomy, for instance, is based upon relationship with sufficient trust so that autonomy is possible. Further, Erikson bases the adult challenges of intimacy and generativity upon sufficient capacities for and meaning in interpersonal relationships. See, e.g., Erik Erikson, *Childhood and Society*, 2d ed. (New York: W. W. Norton, 1963), 247–74. This point will be discussed again in chapter 3.

projects to be part of the larger feminist effort to transform theology and practice in response to contemporary experience. My social location as white, female, married, mother, middle class, Presbyterian clergy, and faculty member in a theological seminary clearly identifies me as a participant in a number of traditional, patriarchal systems and institutions.

This project affirms connections with and encouragement from friends and mentors in the church who have nurtured and challenged me along the way. I have been both nurtured and wounded by the church and its representatives, both empowered and exploited, and no doubt, I too am prone to misusing power, contributing to others' suffering. I have some awareness of my own complicity in oppressive, racist, and classist aspects of the tradition and practices of the church, especially in implicit support of unequal relations of power, knowing that as a white, middle-class person I benefit from that inequity. The problems of racism and economic exploitation in the lives of persons of color and issues specific to lesbian women and gay men are not the focus of this project, but I do not claim that sexism is the most important form of oppression. I attempt to be informed by experiences of persons different from myself while respecting their privilege to name and interpret their own experience.

Among the limits of this project are the hermeneutical choices I have made in selecting particular theologians and theorists in a process of critical and constructive praxis. Some of the feminist theologies and theories of psychotherapy that I utilize can be criticized for bias toward a white, middle-class, heterosexual perspective, while other theologies and theories that inform my work are criticized for being too far outside traditional Reformed theology or mainstream psychotherapy. Current theological debate continues to correct and expand feminist thought so that it does not exacerbate some experiences of oppression while trying to alleviate others. Further, it has become increasingly difficult to generalize about women's experience in an effort to promote advocacy, while respecting individual and group differences that link gender with other categories such as race, class, sexual orientation, and the like. Taking on the challenge of interpreting human experience so that a greater variety of voices can be heard, the literature of theology, therapy, and pastoral theology itself is addressing the multiple oppressions that characterize many lives.[28]

---

28. Several recent works in pastoral theology are contributing to this broader awareness: Carroll Watkins Ali, *Survival and Liberation: Pastoral Theology in the African-American Context* (St. Louis: Chalice Press, 1999); Larry Kent Graham, *Discovering Images of God: Narratives of Care among Lesbians and Gays* (Louisville: Westminster

One of the most persistent issues in feminist theology has been the interpretation of women's experience and the proper relation between experience and tradition as sources for theology. One political theorist has identified four strategies that clarify the hermeneutical choices made in interpreting women's experience. Affirming the centrality of the politics of language, Marilyn Hawkesworth identifies four models of politicization in feminist rhetoric, that is, four ways of talking about women's experience, all aimed at social transformation and each making different assumptions about motivation and dynamics.[29] These four strategies are the rhetoric of oppression, the rhetoric of difference, the rhetoric of reason, and the rhetoric of vision.

Feminist theology emerging from liberation theology, such as the work of Rebecca Chopp, characterizes the rhetoric of oppression. In comparison with other strategies, this rhetoric shifts attention away from individuals toward oppressed groups of persons. In its emphasis on the systemic nature of oppression, it can strengthen the sense of solidarity with others, but it may inadvertently undermine the possibility of imagining women as individual agents who can change their futures. Solidarity with a group of persons may enhance communal agency and action so that interdependence in community is affirmed. However, identification with a group around a single characteristic also has the potential to undermine individual initiative and self-expression and to silence diverse perspectives within the group.

Accounting for women's unique epistemology, or ways of knowing, and capacity for relationality based, in part, on physical experiences and bodily processes specific to women, feminist theorists have employed the rhetoric of difference.[30] The great contribution of this rhetoric is the

John Knox, 1997); Linda Hollies, ed., *Womanistcare: How to Tend the Souls of Women* (Joliet, Ill.: Woman to Woman Ministries, 1991); Joretta L. Marshall, *Pastoral Counseling with Women in Lesbian Relationships* (Louisville: Westminster John Knox, 1997); and James N. Poling, *Deliver Us from Evil: Resisting Racial and Gender Oppression* (Minneapolis: Fortress Press, 1996).

29. Marilyn E. Hawkesworth, *Beyond Oppression: Feminist Theory and Political Strategy* (New York: Continuum, 1990), 110–29.

30. Among pastoral theologians, see, e.g., Patricia H. Davis, *Counseling Adolescent Girls* (Minneapolis: Fortress Press, 1996); Susan Dunlap, *Counseling Depressed Women* (Louisville: Westminster John Knox, 1997); Maxine Glaz and Jeanne Stevenson Moessner, eds., *Women in Travail and Transition: A New Pastoral Care* (Minneapolis: Fortress Press, 1991); Bonnie Miller-McLemore, *Also a Mother: Work and Family as Theological Dilemma* (Nashville: Abingdon, 1994); Bonnie Miller-McLemore and Herbert Anderson, "Gender and Pastoral Care," in *Pastoral Care and Social Conflict*, ed.

revaluation of bodily experience and sensuality, as well as a multitude of forms of nurture, including parenting. But the strategy's potential hazard is a romanticization of womanhood and an overly deterministic positing of women's difference as a function of biology. It may also perpetuate polarization between male and female gender roles by emphasizing complementarity of the sexes and implying biological determinism, thus reducing, rather than enhancing, freedom.

The rhetoric of reason appeals to the belief that oppression is based on ignorance, that reason will triumph and change will occur by an act of will, once persuasion by rational argument has occurred. This rhetoric is a necessary form of thematizing women's oppression, as well as strategizing for change, but it cannot be the only basis for change. It may occur in the form of ongoing dialogue or conversation between equal partners, which presupposes a relationship of solidarity, a kind of dialogical community. Further, the assumption that oppression is based on ignorance does not account for oppression as sin or violation of the relationships God intends. In this way, a rhetoric of reason proceeds on the facile supposition that more information will solve the problem of oppression. Hawkesworth states that feminist scholarship proceeds largely on the basis of this form of rhetoric, but I suggest that feminist theology has developed a more accurate understanding of the force or power of oppression as sin.

The rhetoric of vision relies on myth and symbol, synthesizes certain insights from each of the previous three strategies, and focuses on the imagination as the primary site of ideological struggle. This is familiar ground for much of the constructive work accomplished in feminist theology, given the task of challenging and restoring symbols in a faith tradition. From a literary perspective, this fourth rhetoric consciously engages in the literary production of reality. The rhetoric of vision "recodes" the dominant cultural (or theological) symbols that constitute the key to future social transformation.[31] However, the limits of this postmodern emphasis on language need to be acknowledged, especially the difference between linguistic processes and historical events. Changing language does not necessarily change experience. For instance, changing language in the Bible so that it is more inclusive may inadvertently ren-

---

Pamela D. Couture and Rodney J. Hunter (Nashville: Abingdon, 1995), 99–113; and Jeanne Stevenson Moessner, ed., *In Her Own Time: Religion and Women's Life Cycles* (Minneapolis: Fortress Press, 2000).

31. Hawkesworth, *Beyond Oppression,* 123.

der the culturally bounded aspects of Scripture less visible and thus less accessible for critique.

A typology of feminist rhetoric begins to portray the range of possibilities for how women's experience may be construed and some of the hermeneutical and political implications in describing human experience. The feminist theories in this exploration interpret experience on the basis of all four strategies. Welch's liberation theology emphasizes a rhetoric of oppression and also employs the strategy of vision. McFague's and Brock's theologies emphasize revision as well, through "recoding" the dominant "symbol" of God, our relation to God, and the community formed by Christ. The theories of psychotherapy set forth by Brown and by Ballou and Gabalac politicize experience with the rhetoric of oppression, while the theory of self developed by Gilligan relies heavily on the rhetoric of difference. All of the feminist theologies and theories are forms of feminist scholarship employing the rhetoric of reason.

These distinctions are helpful in using feminist theory in pastoral care and counseling and particularly in respecting the internal coherence and integrity of disciplines used to inform this ministry. As Hawkesworth notes, whether feminists attempt to constitute an identity and a political strategy for women "on the basis of victimization and anger, on the basis of difference and traditional strengths, on the basis of common humanity and rational argument, or on the basis of imagination and myth" has significant implications for action as well as for "the ways in which dominant discourses may attempt to co-opt feminism."[32] Decisions about rhetorical strategy may sound calculated in a discussion of pastoral theology, and yet I would argue that more explicit politicization on the part of feminist theorists is very helpful in exposing the political assumptions in any theology or adjunct theory.

Faithful response, resistance, and connection are themselves "strategic" interpretations of experience, theological notions that emerged through reflection on practice of pastoral care and counseling and that are intended to link experiences with a tradition's themes of re-creation, liberation, and reconciliation. My intention is to open "reflective" space in the ongoing process of praxis, to reconsider the relation between experience and tradition as two sources for pastoral theology, using revised interpretations of each. Whether I have merely co-opted feminist rhetoric into a dominant discourse or have found a useful way to critique and revise assumptions in pastoral care situations remains to be seen.

---

32. Ibid., 128–29.

In chapter 2, I relate problems identified in offering pastoral care to the work of several feminist theologians, focusing on revisions in our sense of response to God and relation to God's creation, a different view of personal, interpersonal, and systemic harm, and the possibility of compassionate community. Chapter 3 discusses several efforts in psychotherapy and psychology and identifies altered understandings of the self and the social and cultural context from this supporting discipline. The resulting revisions in theological and therapeutic perspectives are more fully illustrated in chapter 4 as they inform pastoral responses in specific situations of care, counseling, and consultation. Chapter 5 concludes with reflections on the consequences of the revisioning process and the importance of neither overestimating nor underestimating our part in reflecting what God has done and anticipating what God is calling forth in particular situations of care.

Chapter Two

Contributions from Feminist Theology

Liberation and feminist theologies provide a much needed resource for faith seeking fuller understanding of God's presence and activity and for interpreting structures of contemporary sin and suffering. These theologies offer imaginative reconstructions of our relation to God and practices of faith in response to God that enable caregivers to hear and begin to understand alternative expressions of faith, particular longing for justice, and what God's compassion might look like in the words and images of persons in need. In all their variety, these theological revisions emphasize prophetic themes from Hebrew Scripture and the liberating and reconciling actions of Jesus in relation to persons who were desperately poor or ill, excluded from community by social rules or custom, and his call to repentance and belief in the new creation he portrayed in parables. Liberation and feminist theologies have found a way to understand and seek change in situations of oppression on the basis of faith in the One to whom Scripture bears witness and to expand the capacity of caregivers to respond effectively to diverse forms of suffering.[1] As a source for pastoral theology and reflection on situations of care and counseling, liberation and feminist theologies contribute revisions in our sense of identity and

---

1. The interpretation of Scripture that informs this project may be characterized as "divine message in human forms of thought," one of three general models of interpretation discussed in the study document *Biblical Authority and Interpretation* (Louisville: Office of the General Assembly, Presbyterian Church (U.S.A.), 1982). Emerging in a situation of theological diversity in the 1960s and 1970s, this model emphasizes the function of the Bible and the saving message of Scripture as the Word of God, "with closest attention to the human words, and to the historical and cultural context in which they were originally written. Openness to the Holy Spirit's leading, as well as the tools of scholarship, implemented in faith and love, must be operative to yield the application of the message, especially in areas of controversy." Ibid., 43. This model is particularly open to the social sciences, as they provide insights for understanding Scripture, and to human relational metaphors rather than propositional statements, as they describe God's communication.

purpose in response to God who creates and re-creates, liberates from bondage, and has promised the reconciliation of all creation.

In this chapter, I offer critical assessments of selected feminist theologies in order to think through theological assumptions in pastoral care and counseling, to suggest revisions in the practice of this ministry, and to attend to the practical consequences of a caring response. The sections to follow explore what feminist theology has to say about faithfulness to God and the effects of how relation to God is described, resistance to harm as one way of making justice, and compassionate, interdependent connections with others as part of our purpose. First, however, I will identify several concerns in drawing from feminist and liberation theologies as a focus for the assessment of these contributions to pastoral care. Critical perspectives are themselves subject to critique, particularly as they have aided or impeded practice of ministry. Reflecting the praxis orientation discussed in the preceding chapter, naming these concerns and the ways they are encountered in practice is part of what constitutes pastoral care as a work in progress—a place with windows open and door ajar. I conclude the chapter with a brief summary of the implications of selected feminist theologies for pastoral care.

One way of defining "theology" is "faith seeking understanding" and asking questions about the correspondence of the proclamation and practice of the church to the truth of God's revelation in Jesus Christ as attested in Scripture. Does the church express the whole of that truth, representing God as a living reality in the present context in a way that leads to transforming praxis in personal and social life?[2] As Daniel Migliore notes, the further issue of the location from which these questions are asked—church, academy, or society—is also inescapable and discloses whether or not answers are given only by the privileged or dominant group. The praxis orientation of most liberation and feminist theologies attempts to address this question by critiquing theology and interpreting Scripture based, in part, on the experience of persons who are oppressed.

As I have tried to appropriate feminist theological perspectives into practice of ministry, specifically in response to particular experiences of suffering encountered in care and counseling, three issues have emerged. First, feminist theological perspectives are concerned with analysis of

---

2. The four questions about truth, wholeness, present intelligibility, and practical expression of the gospel are drawn from Daniel L. Migliore's discussion of the task of theology in *Faith Seeking Understanding: An Introduction to Christian Theology* (Grand Rapids: Eerdmans, 1991), 9–13.

power and enhancing freedom but do not often emphasize God's power in terms of freedom and transcendence. Efforts to overcome a dualistic split between God's immanence and transcendence serve a useful purpose in moving beyond spatial representations, and yet we cannot ignore God's freedom. Feminist theology understands *sin* in terms of the distortions of power in patriarchal society, particularly power misused as dominance and the suffering that results, and liberation from these embedded distortions is the vision of the good. The pragmatic focus on the consequences of the church's proclamation and practice is also a major contribution.

At the same time, when the mystery of God's freedom and chosen incarnation is lost, this limits, rather than expands, possibilities for human activity and response. In pastoral practice, I have come to see that highlighting God's active liberation of the oppressed does remind us of God's freedom and initiative in creation and in relation to the power arrangements of any society. Yet I contend that liberation is a crucial, but incomplete, portrayal of God's redemptive action; continued attention to God's work in re-creation and reconciliation provides a fuller account.[3]

Careseekers and caregivers may recall God's activity as power bringing order out of chaos, creating all things and attributing identity to them, sustaining and guiding creation, judging and forgiving humanity. We remember God's power calling persons out of bondage into the freedom of covenant relationship, a relationship characterized by God's steadfast love and the particular identity and practices that are to shape the lives of persons in response to God. Scripture also reminds us of the perpetual human tendency to abandon the freedom of a covenant life and relationship for the sake of some other commitment or loyalty. In Hebrew Scripture, God is known to transcend and yet enter into relationship with humanity, setting persons free from bondage and calling them into covenant relationship. As liberation and feminist theologies draw from Scripture and inform ministries of care, we must affirm some sense of God as known and yet unknowable, even as we try to understand God's actions in creation and intimate relation in covenant.

Theologies that emphasize human liberation without also adequately affirming God's freedom are less likely to attend to how the liberated are

---

3. Migliore notes that theologies of liberation have enhanced understanding of God's redemptive activity not only as a reconciling event but also as a history of liberation: "If reconciliation emphasizes the purpose and goal of God's activity, liberation emphasizes the process through which that goal is attained." Migliore, *Called to Freedom: Liberation Theology and the Future of Christian Doctrine* (Philadelphia: Westminster Press, 1980), 30.

then to use their freedom or the purposes for which the empowered will then exercise power. As these issues have emerged in particular situations of care, the ambiguity of freedom and power becomes evident when power is misused as dominance by persons who are themselves oppressed or when power is unclaimed or unasserted when it would be possible to do so on behalf of oneself and others. I voice this concern as a person of privilege and acknowledge that I have not experienced the depth of suffering others have on account of misused power.[4] But practice of ministry that is informed by feminist thought calls for an emphasis on and reflection of God's liberating activity balanced by an adequate notion of God's mystery, freedom, and otherness. Further, such theology of God is crucial to the vision that we, through practice of ministry, encourage people to become. For what purpose is freedom enhanced? What vision guides the use of people's newly acquired power? How does human exercise of freedom and power relate to God's freedom in relation to us and all creation?

I address these questions through themes that have emerged in my practice of ministry as a caregiver with careseekers wondering how to be faithful to God, what resistance to harm is warranted, and how to manage their "caughtness" in a complex web of relations. The themes are selective theological interpretations of experience that reflect the mutual influence of caregiver and careseeker, as well as engagement with several feminist theologies. Sallie McFague's personal metaphors of God and the world—God as mother, lover, and friend and the world as God's body—suggest altered perceptions of God that may evoke revised and renewed relation for some. Sharon Welch's work illustrates the limits of a liberation theology that analyzes resistance as exercise of power but does so without sufficient account of God's freedom. At the same time, Welch's thought is quite helpful in identifying appropriate forms of resistance as human action that reflects and anticipates God's initiatives in liberation and reconciliation.

A second problem encountered in utilizing liberation and feminist theology in practice of ministry concerns the relationship between (1) human experience and understanding of Jesus Christ and (2) the tendency to understand Jesus Christ only on the basis of one's own par-

---

4. Ibid., 97. Migliore suggests that as those of us who are privileged become aware of our own bondage, we must differentiate it from the oppression experienced by the poor, distinguishing feelings of frustration and disappointment among the relatively affluent from the mistreatment and victimization of the poor.

ticular experience and perceived need. From a perspective of faith, we respond to Jesus Christ because of God's redemptive action in becoming incarnate and understand ourselves to be reconciled to God and one another through him. At the same time our experience shapes our reception of this gift, and the process of appropriating God's grace and forgiveness occurs in the structures and interconnections specific to our lives. The connection between our experience and Jesus Christ is mutual in the sense that we are interpreted by this person and the witness to his life and work while at the same time we interpret and respond to him as the Christ of faith. For purposes of pastoral theology, knowledge of the historical Jesus on the basis of reconstructions of his life based on Scripture enables many to strengthen coherent identity in response to God.

An emphasis on reconciliation as the purpose of God's action in the incarnation enables us to become more forgiving of ourselves and others and provides a basis for accountability. But an emphasis on reconciliation alone ignores the social effects of Jesus' life and work in his own context, especially as he resisted the social rules and structures that would have prevented him from healing, eating, gathering, and talking with persons considered "outside" his social and religious boundaries. Although God's redemptive activity is well described in the term "reconciliation," the resistance to social structuring of relationship that characterizes many of Jesus' actions may be overlooked without further attention to God's incarnation in terms of resistance and freedom. Further, the tendency to disregard differences among people, including differences in power, in an effort to achieve reconciliation or harmony is evidence of disconnection from what Jesus did in his own time and place as we understand it through biblical and historical study.

A more adequate theological understanding of Jesus Christ includes critical reflection on reconstructions of the historical Jesus in addition to knowledge of Jesus Christ through faith, enabling ministries of pastoral care and counseling to reflect more clearly God's reconciling and liberating action in Jesus Christ. I use Rita Nakashima Brock's revisioning of Christology in part to demonstrate the hazards of a spirit Christology that does not adequately address the relation between the historical Jesus and the Christ of faith. In the discussion to follow, I assess the effects of this limitation and point toward a more adequate understanding of God's redemption in terms of the themes of this project.

The third and final issue to be noted in drawing from feminist theology to inform care and counseling is an inadequate theory of self, or theological anthropology as it is sometimes called. Feminist theology offers perspective on the distortions of power in the structures of patriarchal society, but these distortions are internalized within our psychic structure as well as interwoven in social structures. Critical psychological theory is necessary in addition to critical social theory in order to analyze distortions of power and to begin to suggest how these can be changed. For pastoral theology, this means attending to challenges of faithfulness, resistance, and connection in both personal and social realms, to individuals as well as communal interconnections. While I disagree with an overemphasis on spirit Christology, Brock has taken an unusual tack among feminist theologians in her exploration of individual brokenness and the need for self-critical awareness. In addition to analyzing the systemic structure of sin in patriarchal society, Brock is informed by the work of psychoanalytic object relations theory as interpreted by Alice Miller. Using Miller's notion of the split between true self and false self to understand how misused power becomes internalized in the structures of the self, Brock acknowledges the ambiguity of power and calls for empathy with self and others, and even with patriarchal society itself. Hers is an important contribution to a theory of self and pastoral theological anthropology. I use Brock's work to focus on the intrapsychic, interpersonal, and systemic structures of sin and suffering from a theological perspective and assess her perspective on the interdependent connections made possible by God in Jesus Christ.

Metaphors of Relation to God

Particular situations of pastoral care and counseling often include the challenge of faithfulness and the questions of to whom, to what, and how to be faithful. In pastoral ministry, a careseeker's desire to be faithful to God is frequently at issue and may be viewed as an element of both the personal situation of the careseeker and the larger context of pastoral care as a ministry of the church. In my practice of ministry in the local church, most instances of care were with people known across a breadth of experiences in the life of the church, meaning I could assume some shared language of faith and more easily clarify differences and predict practices of faith. Simple queries about how a person views a problematic situation from a faith perspective, or how someone thinks God views a current dilemma, can be helpful invitations to call forth the challenges of individual and corporate faithfulness. Pastoral care includes and encourages forms of worship nourished by Scripture, prayer, and sacrament, and these practices of faith in response to God are the central features of forming and maintaining coherent identity in relation to God. Many instances of pastoral care involve a straightforward evoking of the resources of faith in the face of illness, loss, broken relationships, or life transition, and support through these experiences validates the struggle even as it affirms and embodies faith in God, who suffers with us. The language of discipleship and vocation is a way to talk about what God would have us do in order to be faithful.

In some situations of need, however, personal identity is more fragmented, and traditional symbols for God are no longer credible in relation to experience. In such situations, an adequate pastoral response to suffering involves exploration of an alternative, and yet appropriate, witness to Christian faith.[5] Caregivers may also function in situations where faithfulness is not so evident an issue for a careseeker or when the careseeker and caregiver hold widely divergent views about God or our responsibility in relation to God. Offering care, counseling, or consultation in these circumstances requires clear negotiation of respective expectations, the nature of care being sought, and the caregiver's openness to and ability in addressing a need without imposing a particular faith perspective or opposing alternative views. Some caregivers insist upon using a particular language of faith in order to maintain their own sense of identity in practice of ministry. If that is the case, the careseeker must know of the caregiver's insistence so that he or she is free to engage in the process or to request a referral. But it is safe to assume that most situations in which care is offered involve a diversity of notions about what constitutes faithfulness, and few traditions of faith are singular enough to preclude a variety of interpretations of our relation to God.

Letty Russell characterizes faithful relation to God as partnership with God as our Creator and continuing source of life, as our Liberator who sets the captives free, and as our Advocate continually present with us as a witness.[6] Avoiding personal metaphors for God, she chooses instead to speak in trinitarian metaphors for God's saving activity in the world as

---

5. In her discussion of method in theology, Pamela Dickey Young has identified two criteria for evaluating theological claims that are both feminist and Christian: the norm of appropriateness, that is, whether or not a claim is appropriate to the Christian tradition, and the norm of credibility, evaluating a claim as intellectually and practically credible. She maintains that the two criteria must be held together in forming a Christian, feminist theology. Young, *Feminist Theology/Christian Theology: In Search of Method* (Minneapolis: Fortress Press, 1990), 73–93.

6. Letty Russell, *The Future of Partnership* (Philadelphia: Westminster Press, 1979), 28–33.

Creator, Liberator, and Advocate. The notion of partnership, however, is an interpersonal metaphor that emerged from Russell's own work as a pastor and her participation in conversation with women from all parts of the world about where liberation leads us. The eschatological framework within which Russell explores partnership begins from the point of view of the new creation and what God intends us to become in Jesus Christ, "a new focus of relationship in a common history of Jesus Christ that sets persons free for others."[7] Russell explores partnership with God through stewardship of the new creation and partnership with others through lifestyles, church community life, ministry, and education. But her discussion of partnership with God, particularly God's freedom "for us and from us," is the focus here.

Russell describes the experiences of many women and men who lived in East Harlem in New York City, where she served as a pastor:

> Those who find themselves in situations of political, social, or personal oppression know deep down in spoken and unspoken ways that they are searching for how it would feel to be free. As they refuse to let their humanity be destroyed and struggle toward liberation in whatever their concrete situation of oppression may be, both individuals and groups look to the God of the exodus and of the resurrection. They look for a God who has known suffering and 'Godforsakenness' and has conquered the power of evil through suffering love.[8]

An understanding of God in Jesus Christ as the Liberator helped many as they found small signs of freedom in the midst of substandard housing, bondage in addiction, and economic poverty because they believed new life had begun in Christ. They were strengthened to receive the gift of freedom and to use it even in small ways by God's Spirit, understood not only as Comforter but as Advocate carrying on God's liberating action in their lives. They came to new understanding of God as Creator, whose act of creation included them and gave them worth and who invited them to share in re-creation by caring for the world and society. In fact, Russell describes God as a "humanist," in the sense of being prohuman, and claims that we, too, are called to be humanists, contradicting present realities of suffering, want, hunger, and injustice so that humanity may be re-created.

In her discussion of our relation to God, Russell suggests that we look at how God works in the world in order to discover what we are to do. Part of being "prohuman" is acknowledging our own need to be set free

---

7. Ibid., 16.
8. Ibid., 33.

from personal and social sin that separates us from ourselves, others, and God. Partnership with God also includes advocacy as we use our personal resources, economic power, and social power on behalf of others so that our efforts "take part with Christ" as signs of God's new creation. Russell defends her notion of God's utopia seen in both the "old" and new creation and our purpose as agents of this promised future called to live as small signs of that future. She commends a search for identity, not in psychological theories or in personal or social history, but in God who questions and addresses:

> If we turn to the Bible, asking the question Who am I? we are frequently startled by the point of view we find. For Scripture begins from the other end. It is God who questions and addresses us. God asks Adam, "Where are you?" and Cain, "Where is Abel your brother?" (Gen. 3:9; 4:9). The divine initiative is clear in the stories of Moses, the fugitive from justice: "I will be with you"; Mary, the humble young woman: "Hail, O favored one"; and Jesus, the rabbi, "This is my beloved Son" (Ex 3:12; Luke 1:28; Mark 9:7). The clue the Bible gives is this: What we are is related to the mystery of God's deciding to be with us.[9]

In Russell's view, the utopia or new creation in which we are called to participate is not a spatial reality or "place" or an expression of God's presence above, outside, or within us, but a temporal reality. The new creation is an expression of God's presence in history and with us, and yet it is also "beyond history and ahead of us."[10]

In contrast to Russell's emphasis on temporal reality, McFague has expressed urgent concern for spatial reality and our sense of "place" as members (with all creation) of God's body. In her earlier work, McFague set forth models of God as mother, lover, and friend in the context of the world as God's body and contended that they are more appropriate for our time than familiar models of God as lord, king, and patriarch with the world as his realm.[11] Her "thought experiment" is intent upon "re-

---

9. Ibid., 44.

10. Russell discusses the historicity of human beings in the sense of "transeunce," a form of the word "transient," from the Latin *transire*, "to go beyond." In this sense we operate or go beyond ourselves in order to become ourselves. As she notes, existentialists describe this as the human need for transcendence and identify hope as the driving force behind what it is to be human. But Russell commends the term "transeunce" because "the emphasis is on the beyond in history and existence, and not the beyond, above or outside of history. The relatedness of humans is always situated in history, and God's relatedness takes place in and through history." Ibid., 48.

11. Sallie McFague, *Models of God: Theology for an Ecological, Nuclear Age* (Phila-

mythologizing" Christian faith so that contemporary experience is more adequately interpreted in the faith community in our time. She suggests that these models are metaphors with staying power, retaining an "is and is not" quality and made as a likely account rather than a definition:

> The assumption here is that all talk of God is indirect: no words or phrases refer directly to God, for God-language can refer only through the detour of a description that properly belongs elsewhere. To speak of God as mother is to invite us to consider some qualities associated with mothering as one partial but perhaps illuminating way of speaking of certain aspects of God's relationship to us. It also assumes, however, that many other metaphors may qualify as partial but illuminating grids or screens for this purpose.[12]

As McFague explores the models for God, she addresses three issues in relation to each: What sort of divine love is suggested by each model? What kind of divine activity is implied by this love? What does each kind of love say about existence in our world? Through this exploration, McFague systematically develops an understanding of the God-world relationship. The model of God as mother suggests a creative sort of divine love (*agape*), creative activity of God, and justice as a dimension of Christian discipleship. The model of God as lover suggests salvific love (*eros*) that is the passionate manifestation or incarnation of divine love for us, implying the saving activity of the divine and suggesting healing as a dimension of our discipleship. The third model of God as friend suggests sustaining love (*philia*) as "the immanent, companionable love of God who continues always with us as we work together toward the fulfillment of all," implying the sustaining activity of the divine and suggesting companionship or *philia* as a dimension of our discipleship.[13] Faithfulness, according to McFague's models of God, would mean "commitment to the impartial continuation of life in its many forms, the healing and reunification of

---

delphia: Fortress Press, 1987), xiii. McFague affirms the influence of liberation and feminist thought in her theology but might object to the adjectival qualification of hers or any theology as feminist, black, Third World, etc. She contends that any theology emerges from a concrete, social context, identifies what the authors believes the central vision of Christianity to be, and offers insights that emerge in part because of special perspective: "The crucial difference between these new theologies and classical theology is that for the first time they are coming from women, from people of color, and from the poor." Ibid., 46–47.

12. Ibid., 34.

13. Ibid., 92.

all dimensions of life, and the sharing of the basic needs of life as well as its joy."[14]

In her later work, McFague's stated purpose for an organic model of ecological theology is to see dimensions of the relation of God and the world that we have not seen before and for us to think and act as if bodies matter.[15] The model suggests a way to rethink humanity's place in the larger scheme of things, a "postpatriarchal, Christian theology for the twenty-first century," as McFague states it, offering a significant contribution to pastoral theological reflection and fostering faithfulness through pastoral care.[16] McFague is careful to identify her theology within the monistic track of historical theology, "presuming the basic oneness of all of reality, including the unity of God and the world."[17] Such theology tends to be cosmological and sees salvation as "the ongoing healing of the divided body of our world which we, with God, work at together."[18]

McFague contrasts the monistic model with the dominant track of historical theology, the "monarchical" model, which is characterized by a different understanding of the God-world relationship. Viewing God's activity as redeeming rebellious humanity, the monarchical model assumes an "asymmetrical dualism" in the relation between God and the world. McFague acknowledges that this model is so pervasive that many assume it to be "the way things are," rather than a model or representation of God and the world. In a critique of this model, she identifies three major flaws: God is distant from the world, relates only to the human world, and controls that world through domination and benevolence.[19] McFague's monistic (or more precisely, panentheistic) model assumes a God-world relationship in which "all things have their origins in God and nothing exists outside God, though this does not mean that God is reduced to these things."[20] Within the metaphor of the world as God's body, sin is refusal to be part of the body, to realize one's interdependence with all that is and "the special part we are" as a reflection of God, rather than a kind of disloyalty against God, as in the monarchical model.

Models of God that evoke closeness, intimacy, and personal relation

---

14. Ibid., 92.
15. Sallie McFague, *The Body of God: An Ecological Theology* (Minneapolis: Fortress Press, 1993), viii.
16. Ibid., x.
17. McFague, *Models of God*, 93–95.
18. Ibid., 15.
19. Ibid., 63–69.
20. Ibid., 72.

are a significant and helpful shift in focus, especially when God has been viewed as distant, uninvolved, or unaffected, with sovereign power as dominant and capricious. Making room for alternative understandings that depict God as passionately involved in the world and God's power and activity as creative, saving, and sustaining relativizes predominant views and may be especially effective in shaping responsiveness with persons who have come to assume God's absence or apathy in relation to their lives. McFague's model also prevents privatizing faith through the notion of "recentering," locating our lives in the web of interdependent relations that constitute God's creation, an element in her revision that is among the most helpful for pastoral theologians and caregivers nurturing faith and its individual and communal expression. Such alternative views provide a broader range of vision for pastoral ministry oriented by a praxis method. Careseekers' voices and views are privileged in the caring process, and predominant views are not simply imposed in a manner that overtakes a careseeker's authority and agency. Working from a theological "location" with a sufficiently diverse range of viewpoints enables caregivers to use their power in a collaborative manner and yet proclaim or affirm faith.

My own practice of ministry promotes a combination of personal or intimate relationship with God, as well as a firm sense of God's freedom in relation to the world and the world's freedom in response to God. Efforts to draw a fuller distinction between Creator and creation and still avoid the sense of God's power as domination or disconnected from grace are carried out in dialogue with careseekers and their respective views. As Migliore has stated,

> The idea of God as an uninvolved and distant creator (a typical character-ization in the Western philosophical tradition) is totally inadequate from a biblical perspective. On the other hand, the newly revived panentheistic description of the world as God's body, while emphasizing the intimacy of the relationship between God and the world, fails to depict appropriately either the freedom of God in relation to the world or the real otherness and freedom of the world.[21]

Combining the elements of creative freedom and intimacy of relation more accurately imagines God's power and activity and fosters our re-sponse to God in a manner that affirms interdependence and responsible action in relation to other persons and creation itself. Adequate metaphors for relation to God represent God's activity in a way that calls forth faith-

---

21. Migliore, *Faith Seeking Understanding,* 94.

fulness and that represents individual and communal agency as the means for responsible participation that anticipates God's new creation.

Resistance and Solidarity in Suffering

In this section, I focus specifically on resistance as a response to sin and suffering, a reflection of God's transcendence, and a kind of anticipatory freedom. Resistance can be a sign of freedom and evidence of creativity and vitality, and we can use theological criteria to determine what forms of resistance are to be encouraged by pastoral caregivers. I have been surprised at the effects of identifying even small acts of resistance or courage as such with careseekers who have minimized their efforts. Further, exploring appropriate resistance as a reflection of God's liberative justice can be heartening for those discouraged by intractable circumstances.

Welch's theology challenges a ministry of pastoral care and counseling as practice of faith to include more active criticism and resistance to the suffering caused by injustice. In her theology, resistance is opposition to particular configurations of power and knowledge, challenge to particular forms of oppression, and "a refusal to make definitive, pretentious claims to essential or ultimate truth."[22] Welch sees a convergence between the concerns of liberation theologians and the work of Michel Foucault as he analyzes power and the effects of discourse. Foucault understands language as a practice that does not merely reflect reality but produces and shapes reality.[23] As a discursive practice or action, language is a form of power that actively influences and constructs knowledge not only of ourselves and our relationships but of larger systems and institutions as well. Welch applies Foucault's questions to the Christian tradition in order to understand Christianity in terms of its practice, not just in terms of its symbols and doctrines.

Welch interweaves liberative theology and critical theory, holding relativism and skepticism in tension with commitment to change in social structures. In her terms, the elements of a theology of liberation are "relativist limitations of truth-claims and a qualified nihilism" along with "a strong normative claim to identify values and structures that can transform society and end oppression."[24] Welch acknowledges that these elements of

22. Sharon D. Welch, *Communities of Resistance and Solidarity: A Feminist Theology of Liberation* (Maryknoll, N.Y.: Orbis Books, 1985), 18.

23. Michel Foucault, *Power/Knowledge: Selected Interviews and Other Writings, 1972–1977* (New York: Pantheon, 1980), 119.

24. Welch, *Communities of Resistance and Solidarity,* 84.

relativism and normative claim are contradictory and asserts that the tension between the two is necessary for a truly liberative feminist theology. Relativism acknowledges that relationships are shaped by arrangements of power, and Welch identifies ways in which power may be utilized to heal rather than destroy, to free rather than to oppress.

Although I disagree with some aspects of Welch's thought, I take seriously her challenge to an ethic of risk because of her attention to what enables moral action and sustained political resistance in the face of temptations to resignation. Her theology presses ethics beyond or through the realm of discourse to a different sort of relational power and moral action, with a correlative of divine immanence. The ethic of risk is based on "love for the earth, for oneself, for those who are oppressed, and for those who work against oppression."[25] Welch names two steps in a critical theological method. One is choosing a particular focus for the work of theology and looking at how faith functions in that situation, especially the way in which faith "maintains or challenges structures of oppression." She comments on the second step in a critical theological method as

> a search for alternative symbols and structures of religious life that might effectively challenge oppressive manifestations of faith (symbols, rituals, polity, doctrines) and that might meet, in less oppressive ways, some of the needs being met by the problematic religious discourse. The truth of such theological construction is not measured by its coherence or adequacy but by its efficacy in enhancing a particular process of liberation.[26]

Using the method suggested by Welch, a pastoral caregiver would first look at how faith functions in a particular situation and whether it serves to maintain or modify structures of oppression. However, I argue that this judgment cannot be made only on the basis of efficacy in enhancing resistance to oppression because some theological criteria are needed to interpret whether or not resistance is, indeed, liberative. A second step, according to Welch, would be seeking the life of faith or practices of faith that nurture and support resistance to unequal relations of power and a form of human connection and community that supports more equitable

---

25. Sharon D. Welch, *A Feminist Ethic of Risk* (Minneapolis: Fortress, 1990), 172.
26. Ibid., 158. This understanding of theological method is at odds with the method discussed by Young, for instance, in which she identifies norms of appropriateness and credibility relative to the Christian tradition and human experience respectively. According to Young's perspective, Welch collapses the criterion of appropriateness into the criterion of credibility so that, in effect, Welch argues that what liberates is Christian. Young, *Feminist Theology/Christian Theology*, 73–90.

relations. As Welch suggests, the issue is not simply to denounce systems of oppression, exposing their "frailties of practice," but to determine how alternatives may be disclosed and created.[27] Her theological method involves opposition to what is harmful or destructive and support of or alliance with what heals and creates justice.

Welch offers a corrective to any theology that does not reflect upon the efficacy of theological claims in human experience. But I contend that a better balance between efficacy and possibility is needed in order to more adequately understand God. A greater sense of God's freedom would further enhance the possibilities for human effectiveness as people engage in a more hopeful, imaginative, anticipatory sort of activity. What is at stake, in part, is the question of whether we are counting on our efforts to be fully effective in establishing liberation. My argument is that we are responsible for the effectiveness of our efforts and also confident that God's fulfillment of liberation accomplishes something different from and in addition to what we do or imagine.

The "moral wisdom" of authors in the black women's literary tradition is a source for Welch's ethic of risk. She analyzes the narrative works of womanist authors Paule Marshall and Toni Cade Bambara, among others, for clues to the communicative ethic she develops.[28] Acknowledging that as a white woman she cannot speak for the authors, Welch finds in her own work with African American women resources that bring healing and hope. She also notes the danger of romanticizing and simplifying the history of African Americans and a tendency to see only the endurance and not the costs borne by them. She discusses how harmful it is to restrict "the description of Black experience to unrelieved suffering or, at the other extreme, to the continual miracle of collective triumph."[29] The literature from which she draws does not shy away from contradictions or ambiguity in the lives of persons engaged in resistance to oppressive conditions.

Mildred Taylor's portrayal of one African American family, the Logans, is intended as a reminder of the courage of men and women who strug-

---

27. Ibid., 217.

28. Welch draws upon the wisdom from womanist authors of five novels: Paule Marshall's *The Chosen Place, the Timeless People,* Toni Morrison's *The Bluest Eye,* Mildred Taylor's *Roll of Thunder, Hear My Cry,* and *Let the Circle Be Unbroken,* and Toni Cade Bambara's *The Salt Eaters.*

29. Welch, *Feminist Ethic of Risk,* 17, citing Diana T. Meyers and Eva Feder Kittay, eds., introduction to *Women and Moral Theory* (Totowa, N.J.: Rowman and Littlefield, 1987), 3.

gled against racism. As children today hear of the tenacity and persistence of others who have struggled for justice, they understand their own potential strength. One of the most striking features of the Logan family is their deep joy, "a profound affirmation of life expressed in their connections with, and delight in, family, nature, and the African-American community."[30] The children, in particular, understand themselves to be part of the forest and find comfort and a sense of belonging there. Taylor's central character, Cassie Logan, describes this sense of place:

> We grew quiet, and in our silence all the sounds of the day seemed louder. A bee zoomed past trumpeting its presence, and a dragonfly spun in rapid delight above our heads, then flew on in happy celebration. I shaded my eyes with my hands and looked out over the land. The forest, deep greens and shades of brown, the fields looking like a patchwork quilt of growing things, the house, the orchard, the meadowland, were as much a part of me as my arms, my legs, my head.[31]

The sense of belonging and joy in connection with the Logans' community occurs in a context of consistent racist threats to their dignity and to their lives. Taylor sets their story in the Depression era of the South. As Welch notes, the maturity fostered in this family involves an accurate understanding of racism and the dynamics of power it employs, with persistent courage to work toward change even when complete change is not in sight. The family's resistance takes the form of courage and honesty in the face of inadequate school facilities, the danger of lynching, the unlikelihood of justice in the legal system, and the need to be wary of white people in a racist society. Appropriate resistance and a construction of responsible action are based as much on the possibilities they create as on the immediate results they produce. Responsible action "provides partial resolutions and the inspiration and conditions for further partial resolutions by others. It is sustained and enabled by participation in a community of resistance."[32]

A theological vision of "matrix in the beloved community" emerges as an alternative to the "kingdom of God," as Welch engages these narratives, offering hope for sustaining resistance to injustice. Welch contends that the notion of the "kingdom of God" serves to polarize finite and infinite, God and humanity, in a way that renders persons less able to use

---

30. Welch, *Feminist Ethic of Risk,* 71.

31. Mildred Taylor, *Roll of Thunder, Hear My Cry* (New York: Bantam, 1984), 230, cited in Welch, *Feminist Ethic of Risk,* 72.

32. Welch, *Feminist Ethic of Risk,* 75.

their power for changing the status quo. Welch argues that the idea of God's kingdom leads to a "mood of cultured despair" rather than a sustained hope. She sees an alternative way of understanding limited attempts to transform unjust social structures, and to sustain resistance in the face of these limitations, in the work of feminist and womanist authors.[33] In Welch's view, this literature draws distinctions between limits to human well-being caused by injustice and those caused by natural disasters and human conflicts due to difference rather than exploitation. The first set of limits is to be eliminated, but human conflicts other than those caused by exploitation and natural limitations often cannot be removed and are to be survived with creative endurance as conditions of life. For purposes of pastoral care, distinguishing between what must be endured and what can be challenged is an important issue.

An appropriate symbol for a creative response to life's contingencies and resistance to injustice is the "beloved community." In this matrix, Welch sees a basis for the critique of injustice grounded in solidarity with the oppressed, as well as self-criticism and love of oneself. She is careful to distinguish this love from self-sacrifice, understood as loss of self, and interprets solidarity as finding a "larger self" that includes community with others: "Attempts to eradicate injustice are made, yet other limitations of human existence are accepted—the transitoriness of institutions, the need to let go of old pains and embrace new challenges with their attendant pain, and the limits of being finite and dependent on the earth."[34] Welch's exploration of resistance and solidarity is a source for pastoral care because she draws from stories of people who live with dignity and resist oppression and whose partial resistance creates the conditions for further resistance. These stories suggest an orientation toward praxis, tending to the acts of resistance already occurring in lived experience and finding there a basis for concrete hope and communal joy. Such an orientation would suggest paying attention to instances where resistance to domination is taking place, where contradictions are already beginning to be acknowledged, and where incongruities with power systems are already emerging.

Pastoral care and the community from which it is offered could be like the matrix Welch describes, particularly if the power of language

---

33. In addition to the womanist authors of novels, Welch draws from ethicist Katie G. Cannon, "The Black Woman's Literary Tradition as a Source for Ethics," in *Black Womanist Ethics* (Atlanta: Scholars Press, 1988), 75–98.

34. Welch, *Feminist Ethic of Risk,* 159.

to construct reality and shape experience is recognized. Identifying even small acts of courage in the face of oppression or exploitation may contribute to liberation from sin, in the sense that Welch discusses sin in its structural manifestations and as "cultured despair," or resignation in the face of the complexities of injustice. This despair is the abandonment of independent thinking and the inability to act, which Welch sees as the inevitable result of valorization of God's absolute power implicit in the thought of many liberation theologians.[35] Pastoral care with persons who are waiting for God to intervene in a situation, rather than acting to alleviate some suffering, may be much more open to taking this responsibility when a more accurate and sufficient theological interpretation of resistance is suggested. Such interpretation may be offered by the careseeker or by the caregiver or by both.

Despite the many aspects of Welch's theology that contribute to the various ministries of pastoral care, I disagree with her rejection of God's transcendence or being in addition to the human expression of love and critique of injustice in the "beloved community." She understands resistance, in part, as an unwillingness to make definitive, universal claims to truth. Welch's attention to the practical, material notion of truth leads her to confirm the failure of Christian faith understood as a failure of practice as well as thought, a failure to establish its vision of human community. She rejects the type of theological discourse that uses ahistorical or supernatural authorities from Scripture or tradition without acknowledging the "tenuousness, contingency, and partiality"[36] that characterize these sources. However, in her criticisms of the Christian tradition, Welch herself often chooses selective emphasis as, for instance, in focusing on the tradition's devaluing of the body without also noting the meaning of the incarnation as affirmation of human, bodily existence. She chooses to criticize the imperial understanding of God's power but fails to note the self-giving, self-emptying nature of God's power as well. Welch makes a case for a theology of immanence in which the divine is equivalent to human relational power, but I do not find such power, disconnected from God as Creator and Jesus Christ as God incarnate, an adequate source for the love or resistance that Welch commends.

Pastoral care informed by feminist perspectives may lift up resistance as thematic, pointing out the consonance and contradictions between experiences of suffering and what we know of God's presence and ac-

---

35. Ibid., 115.
36. Welch, *Communities of Resistance and Solidarity,* 32.

tivity. Caregivers need awareness of the internalized nature of relations of power, as well as its systemic manifestations, confidence in human action that resists harm, and critical perspective on acts of resistance that are themselves misuses of power.

Connections in Interdependent Community

Connections characterized by interdependence and compassion can reflect and anticipate God's reconciling activity as we know it through Jesus Christ. Pastoral theological reflection on themes from situations of pastoral care continues in this section with a focus on connection and interdependent relations. The faith commitments that inform this reflection are that who we are and what we are to do are known through relation to God and fuller understanding of divine activity in creating, liberating, and reconciling. I contend that self-critical awareness and analysis of systemic structuring of power emerge from this relation in a manner that makes compassionate connection and healthy interdependence more possible. Our identity becomes clearer and our exercise of agency more purposeful through knowledge of Jesus' life, death, and resurrection and by the continuing work of God's Spirit.

I pursue this discussion with the understanding that the historical Jesus as we know him in the reconstructions of research is not the resurrected Christ of faith—the person who was incarnate, crucified, and raised from death—whom we know through faith as a living person glorified in God. One biblical scholar states that the quest for the historical Jesus in modern scholarship is not necessary for and cannot be the object of Christian faith.[37] John P. Meier argues that the quest is very useful for theology, for faith seeking understanding in a contemporary context, in order to remind us of the specificity of the content of Christian faith in persons and events. Further, historical Jesus studies thwart docetic attempts to obscure the humanity of Jesus into an emphasis on his divinity and prevent "domestication" of Jesus for a comfortable, respectable, bourgeois Christianity. Meier contends that study of the historical Jesus subverts not just some ideologies but all ideologies, including liberation theology, and makes it more difficult to reduce Jesus to any "relevant" ideology. I suggest that reconstructions of the historical Jesus that work from an explicit fem-

---

37. The relationship between the historical Jesus and the Christ of faith is discussed by John P. Meier in *A Marginal Jew: Rethinking the Historical Jesus*, vol. 1, *The Roots and the Problem of the Person* (New York: Doubleday, 1991), 196–200.

inist perspective, or that focus on Jesus as a social revolutionary, are among the results of scholarship and contribute to appropriate theological formulation without replacing other reconstructions.[38] I draw from the work of Brock in order to analyze the possibilities and problems of one feminist christological formulation as it contributes to reflection on practice of ministry.

Brock develops her notions of Christology in iconoclastic terms, discussing Jesus Christ as the second branch of the "unholy Trinity" used to reinforce male dominance and suggesting that because Jesus is male, women must enter Christianity through male action and authority.[39] She criticizes Christology that makes separation and disconnection the source of reconciliation and connection, as she interprets traditional doctrines of new life through the death of the Son, Jesus Christ. Brock names this atoning death of the Son as a model of abusive relationships and begins to expose the patriarchal family structure suggested in the "unholy Trinity" of Father, Son, and Holy Ghost.[40] An understanding of Christ as the full incarnation of God/dess in life-giving relationships is Brock's alternative, expanding Christ beyond Jesus of Nazareth. Rather than viewing Christ singly as the Son of God, this alternative Christology offers a different vision of the life-giving power of community as the true power for redemption of human life. Brock's work uses Scripture as a source, examining the life and work of Jesus Christ in the Gospel of Mark, illuminating the liberating and healing spirit in that life and work as it moves us toward forgiving, healing relationships. Using the Gospel for an iconoclastic function, Brock seeks to demystify power as domination and subordination at both personal and political levels, but she sees this "shattering" as only half the story.

Brock states that liberation is only one element in relationships and that iconoclasm remains "too polarizing" to sustain:

---

38. See, e.g., John Dominic Crossan, *The Historical Jesus: The Life of a Mediterranean Jewish Peasant* (San Francisco: HarperSanFrancisco, 1991); and *Jesus: A Revolutionary Biography* (San Francisco: HarperSanFrancisco, 1994); or Elisabeth Schüssler Fiorenza, *In Memory of Her: A Feminist Theological Reconstruction of Christian Origins* (New York: Crossroad, 1983); and *Jesus—Miriam's Child, Sophia's Prophet: Critical Issues in Feminist Christology* (New York: Continuum, 1995).

39. Rita Nakashima Brock, *Journeys by Heart: A Christology of Erotic Power* (New York: Crossroad, 1988), xii.

40. Pastoral theologian James N. Poling also offers critical perspective on the atonement in his work *The Abuse of Power: A Theological Problem* (Nashville: Abingdon, 1991).

> The rebellion against paternalism and oppression is an important step of
> anger, but being stuck in anger can lead to a rigid self-righteousness that is
> not self-critical or aware of an unconscious reenactment of power over
> others. The shattering of dominant power must be accompanied by a
> move toward self-awareness and self-affirmation.[41]

A focus only on external political and social systems prevents critical self-awareness and self-affirmation that may offer "liberating insights," and alternative relationships in a community of mutual liberation are necessary. This explicit move toward self-critical awareness, challenging the broken heart's tendency toward controlling power and defensive rigidity, distinguishes Brock's effort. She uses the adjunct discipline of psychology in order to explore damage to self that is a consequence of patriarchy, specifically the object relations theory of psychoanalyst Alice Miller.[42] Gaining access to the "true" self is the process of treatment in Miller's theory, including the feelings and experiences from early childhood that have been repressed in order to protect the parental introjects and to avoid the pain associated with early punishment and humiliation.

Brock uses Miller's notion of "true self" as parallel to her own term "heart," a holistic metaphor for the human self and our capacity for intimacy, a unity of body, spirit, reason, and passion.[43] Miller's notion of "false self" is then equivalent to a "broken heart" in Brock's reformulation. Miller suggests that children, because of their dependency, produce false selves that mirror adult needs and neuroses, losing touch with feelings about sexuality, sensuality, and anger. The true self, on the other hand, is the tactile, sensory, feeling self that does not repress intense feelings or need to reject bodily vulnerability or sensuality. Miller is also very interested in exposing the harmful effects of controlling and punishing behavior by parents in order to change the way children are raised and to stop the uncritical perpetuation of violence and power as dominance from generation to generation.

Brock's appropriation of psychoanalytic theory is not entirely clear. For example, how does she avoid the potential for the destructive effect of expressing intense feelings? What guidelines would she use to

---

41. Brock, *Journeys by Heart*, xiii.

42. Alice Miller, *The Drama of the Gifted Child: The Search for the True Self* (New York: Harper Collins, 1981); and *For Your Own Good: Hidden Cruelty in Child-Rearing and the Roots of Violence*, 3d ed. (New York: Noonday, 1990).

43. As Brock uses the term "reason" in defining heart, she apparently intends, not the Aristotelian focus of a rational, cognitive process of the mind, but something more like discernment or the "deeper" logic of the heart.

assure constructive expression of feeling, while avoiding misuse of power? Brock argues for demystification of power as domination and subordination, and she believes this will happen in relationships in "Christa/ Community," but she does not discuss the therapeutic or healing process by which this would occur. She doesn't develop the means by which a community calls forth or invites expression of true self or heart, and it is not clear whether one needs psychotherapy to be sufficiently healed of family of origin issues so that expression of false self is not replicated in community. Though Brock draws from Miller's work, which is rooted in psychoanalytic thought, the absence of reference to treatment or therapy in Brock's discussion implies that being in community will itself lead persons to discover and express true self. I would contend that *Jesus Christ* is the "link" who makes possible expression of true self and empathic, interdependent connection as a reflection and anticipation of God's reconciling presence, but Brock may not view Jesus Christ as *living* in this sense. For purposes of pastoral theology, the remaining question is how the community she describes is more reflective of Christ's presence and able to resist the sin of misusing power any more than the traditional church that claims foundation in this redemptive and corrective presence.

On the other hand, turning patriarchy "inside out," as Brock states it, rather than turning oppressed and oppressor "upside down," represents a different position or relation with respect to patriarchal power: "I am seeking to turn patriarchy inside out, to reveal its ravaged, faint, fearful, broken heart, and to illuminate the power that heals heart. It is a power that allows the touching of heart to heart, a healing and touching that guide us toward a greater experience of the sacred in life."[44] Turning the heart of patriarchy inside out in order to respond to its brokenness suggests a different kind of connection with and perception of structures and systems, with other persons as we imagine their interior experience of brokenness, and with our own broken heart or fragmented self. As I interpret her statement, patriarchy is a kind of brokenness, or sin, in all of us, internalized within each fragmented self and structured in our relationships. Turning the heart of patriarchy inside out would then mean exposing this brokenness not just in some persons but in all people and acknowledging that this brokenness conditions each inner self, interpersonal relationship, and social structure.

The link or interconnection between these dimensions implied in Brock's statement is brokenness, or sin. She discusses sin as historically

---

44. Brock, *Journeys by Heart*, xv.

and socially produced, distinguishing it from notions of original sin. For Brock, sin is "a symptom of the unavoidably relational nature" of human existence:

> If we begin with an understanding that we are intimately connected, constituted by our relationships ontologically, that is, as a basic unavoidable principle of existence, we can understand our brokenness as a consequence of our relational existence. This ontological relational existence, the heart of our being, is our life source, our original grace. But we are, by nature, vulnerable, easily damaged, and that vulnerability is both the sign of our connectedness and the source of the damage that leads us to sin.[45]

In Brock's schema, it is brokenheartedness and damage that are to be healed rather than willful disobedience or evil that are to be punished. Her analysis of sin as brokenheartedness and damage is appealing in its tenderness because, it would seem, broken hearts can be mended and damage repaired, perhaps largely through our compassionate efforts. But this view of sin is partial, and a fuller understanding would include willful disobedience and evil that not only damage but destroy.

Problems encountered in situations of pastoral care call for more than demystification in order to address destructive powers within ourselves and other persons and systems. Brock commends relationships in community that support and develop the "play space" to demystify destructive powers, and I would claim that pastoral relationships may develop such safe space. But a distinction between the limited, human community formed through faith in Jesus Christ and the divine being understood as the triune God is necessary precisely because of the brokenness that exists in community, whether it is the institutional church or some other form of faith gathering. Such a distinction allows those who have been harmed in Christian community to continue working to address the causes of damage and manifestations of sin in the institutional church and frees even those of us who represent the church to point toward God's freedom to judge and correct destructive power. The alternative Christology Brock develops is centered, not in Jesus, but in relationship and community as the "whole-making, healing center of Christianity," which she calls "Christa/Community." In using this term, she intends to shift the focus of salvation away from heroic individuals, to shatter conventional ways of thinking with new images, and to affirm her conviction about the sacredness of community:

---

45. Ibid., 7.

> Jesus participates centrally in this Christa/Community, but he neither brings erotic power into being nor controls it. He is brought into being through it and participates in the co-creation of it. Christa/Community is a lived reality expressed in relational images. Hence Christa/Community is described in the images of events in which erotic power is made manifest. ... What is truly christological, that is, truly revealing of divine incarnation and salvific power in human life, must reside in connectedness and not in single individuals.[46]

While I affirm and build on elements of Brock's revision of Christology, her effort demonstrates the partiality of deideologization of Scripture in the method of liberation theology. As suggested earlier, if attention to the historical Jesus serves the purpose of subverting any ideology, how does one proceed in exploring the creative, liberative, and reconciling activity of God from a praxis orientation in a manner that acknowledges the freedom of God? How does a pastoral theologian reflect on practice of ministry and the needs encountered in pastoral work without reducing God's activity to correspond with a caregiver's response to immediate need? Brock's revisioning of Christology is intended as a corrective to portrayals of Jesus that disallow the influence of his context and community. But if a focus on the community generated through him excludes distinguishable relation to Jesus Christ as living person, the liberative function of the reformulation effort is not well served. Without losing the corrective of Brock's work, further exploration of the relation between the Jesus of history and the object of Christian faith may be helpful.

According to Meier, the historical Jesus and the Christ of faith are different because the various portraits of the historical Jesus are contradictory and the object of Christian faith cannot be an idea or a scholarly reconstruction: "For contemporary Christology, this means that faith in Christ today must be able to reflect on itself systematically in a way that will allow an appropriation of the quest for the historical Jesus into theology. The historical Jesus, while not the object or essence of faith, must be an integral part of modern theology."[47] For Meier, in the realm of faith and theology the "real Jesus" is the risen Lord to whom we have access through faith. Meier argues that studies of the historical Jesus should be appropriated into theology because it reminds persons of faith of the specific content of our faith in a particular person.

---

46. Ibid., 52.
47. Meier, *Marginal Jew,* 196–200.

Meier distinguishes between (1) "faith-knowledge" of Jesus as the object of faith (the crucified, resurrected, living person with whom the believer has a relationship), (2) the existential interest and commitments of theology about the "historic" Jesus (which may occur with or without faith-knowledge), and (3) the analysis of empirical data regarding the "historical" Jesus that occurs in the historical-critical effort (through "purely scientific means"). He insists that as a scholar he brackets, but does not betray, that first kind of faith-knowledge in order to pursue the scientific method of study. Meier acknowledges, however, that one cannot adequately disentangle the "historic Jesus" from the "historical Jesus": "In reality, the one flows too much into the other. While the scholar may try to prescind from a specifically Christian or ecclesiastical commitment, a more general 'existential commitment,' a concern about what Jesus may mean for human life today, necessarily energizes the historical quest."[48]

A scholar may foresee or anticipate something on the basis of the gift of faith, but it is a more general commitment to what Jesus means for us now that energizes historical Jesus studies. We can make a similar point for pastoral theologians who bring faith commitments to the task of reflection on practice of ministry. The history of practical theology itself may be traced along the lines of integrating or dichotomizing theory and practice and the continuing effort of pastoral theology to unify ecclesial interest in the care of souls with disciplined reflection upon relationship with God.[49] I understand faith or faith-knowledge of Jesus to be a very specific gift of relationship with a person who has a particular history of life, crucifixion, death, and resurrection, a relationship that brings coherence to life, identifying who we are and what we are to do.

Pastoral care engages situations that may call for imagining God in unconventional terms in order to recover an appropriate sense of God's creative, liberative, or reconciling activity and to "reconnect" with and re-

---

48. Ibid., 31.

49. I refer to the early work of Schleiermacher, whose efforts to justify theology alongside the other "sciences" in the academy included an emphasis on the unity of theological scholarship in three areas of study: biblical/historical studies, systematic/philosophical theology, and practical theology. A contemporary issue for practical theology is the tendency to reduce this area of study to techniques in a manner that separates it from disciplined reflection upon relationship with God, rather than maintaining the unity and mutual influence of the three areas. For a summary of this problem, see a work edited by James O. Duke and Howard Stone, *Friedrich Schleiermacher, Christian Caring: Selections from Practical Theology* (Philadelphia: Fortress Press, 1988).

spond to God's presence. Caregivers may emphasize the controversial or social revolutionary actions of Jesus as he included and reached out to persons usually excluded or oppressed in his society and do so in a manner that fosters faithfulness and interdependence in community. Pastoral ministry may include response to brokenheartedness in personal, interpersonal, and systemic dimensions and look toward the possibility of interconnections that are "changed" in Jesus Christ. These insights from theological exploration are important with persons who are enduring situations in which their influence is limited or with persons who suffer in isolation, unable to imagine that change is possible within and around them. Pastoral theologians may be informed by reconstructions of the historical Jesus in order to expand notions about the "historic" Jesus, portrayals that may or may not affect the person's perception of the Christ with whom he or she has a relationship of faith. Representations of the historical Jesus may inform our theological understanding of the Christ of faith but do not replace such relationship or faith commitment.

Implications for Pastoral Theology

Exploring feminist revisions in theology highlights several concerns for caregivers, which I summarize around the three issues identified in the beginning of this chapter: an adequate theology of and relation to God, the relation between our experience and our knowledge of Jesus Christ, and an adequate theory of self, or theological anthropology. The three issues are, of course, interrelated and far broader than this discussion reflects, but a selective focus on key points raised through praxis—practice of pastoral care, reflection on sources of knowledge, altered practice, and so on—denotes the constructive struggle of pastoral theology.

Caregivers make important choices about the language and images we use to characterize relationship to God and God's relation to the world, reflecting a more or less adequate theology of God that corresponds to Scripture, represents God as a living reality in the present context, and leads to transformation in personal and social life. In many instances, careseekers also bring an operative theology of God to bear in their situation of need and are invited to explore their understanding of God's presence and activity in collaboration with the caregiver.[50] In this collaborative con-

---

50. I have discussed this interaction of careseeker and caregiver in another project, "Collaborative Pastoral Conversation," in *Brief Strategies in Pastoral Counseling,* ed. Howard Stone (Minneapolis: Fortress Press, 2001).

versation, the traditional language of faith, which characterizes God in terms of love, sovereignty, grace, judgment, and the like, may serve purposes of care and counseling quite well. Yet some situations of care call for alternative language, and feminist theology makes a significant contribution in expanding these options for constructing or reconstructing a careseeker's sense of what constitutes a faithful response to God. Both de-ideologization and remythologizing of Scripture may be involved in the process, particularly if a parishioner or client has a passage of Scripture or biblical figure that resonates with a current dilemma.

In one situation of pastoral counseling, the client and I identified what her experiences of community had been and analyzed the power differences in these relationships. We named what was broken and in need of healing where possible and what connections were sacred and in need of further attention. We considered additional group experiences in which she could participate, where her anger and vulnerability might be supported and understood. Because this client, as a young woman, had experienced conversion and claimed Jesus Christ as her Savior, we explored the meaning of this experience for her at that time, the current shape of her relationship with Jesus, and how she imagined Jesus as Savior in the future. She said it was very difficult for her to say, "Jesus Christ is my Savior," because she had assumed her salvation meant protection from physical harm. Because Jesus did not prevent experiences of verbal and physical abuse by her father, she was redefining what her salvation meant.

From my own perspective, God is present with us in suffering and makes resistance to destructive power possible. One outcome of conversation with the client was identifying how she could protect herself from the risk of further abuse as well as manage her own anger differently so that she did not perpetuate this misuse of power in her relationships with others. Another outcome was that she found it difficult to call God "Father" and had begun to use other language to signify her relationship with God. From a theological viewpoint, she made a distinction between God with whom we have relationship and the language or symbol we use to signify God. This distinction afforded the use of language that was more credible in her experience and yet corresponded appropriately as an interpretation of tradition. One consequence of this revision in her language about God was a shift in her sense of possibility and responsibility in her closest relationships, as she clarified what faithfulness meant in response to the living God in her present situation. The intersection of an adequate theology of God, the revised relation of a person's experience to a faith tradition and its practices, and an altered sense of self and interpersonal relationship is, in my view, a remarkably common opportunity in pastoral care and counseling.

The contribution of feminist theology to this process is a willingness to risk a new representation of God as it emerges with careseekers in order to make fuller relationship with and response to God more possible. I have certainly experienced a limit in my own willingness to engage in this risk when a parishioner or client seemed to be rationalizing or justifying harmful behavior by portraying God in a manner that was credible to his or her experience but contradicted the "whole" of God revealed in Jesus Christ. As caregivers who try to be faithful witnesses to the creative, liberating, and reconciling activity of God, we must clarify and explore such contradictions.

Questions of identity in relation to God and purpose in response to God arise in pastoral care when careseekers no longer experience continuity and coherence. If identity means the state of being the same, then disruption in this state can cause brief or prolonged confusion and may open an opportunity for growth in relation to God, who suffers with us. Recall the pastoral vignettes from the preceding chapter. Ray and Janet face the challenge of adaptation to changes in individual family members and may need to revise the family's covenant with one another in order to sustain interdependence and relatively equal accommodation for the sake of justice. Clive faces the unwelcome challenge of a health crisis that may entail adjustments in stress management and some way of affirming his enjoyment of work even as he revalues his health and reconnects with those he loves. The First Community congregation is dealing with its inability to re-create the past and may yet find a way to anticipate an unknown future based on clarity about their identity and purpose in relation to the living God, a God who calls us to venture forth in faith. Many of the women in the single-parent program experienced repeated abuse and continued to participate in relationships that exposed them to further harm. To the extent that they identified themselves with this history, pastoral care encouraged freedom from that aspect of their identity and purposeful action expressing an alternative identity so that change toward safety and health was possible.

Feminist theology as a source of knowledge informing practice of ministry contributes to these or similar situations of care, counseling, or consultation by broadening the language and expression of faith. Caregivers may listen for and speak of God's history of activity as Creator, Liberator, and Advocate and characterize relation to God in more temporal terms of partnership in working with God toward the new creation.

Careseekers may speak of God's love or the longing for such love in personal metaphors that connote God's creative, saving, or sustaining love and be invited to say more about how they experience or imagine God's activity in their specific situation based on such love. Further, encouragement to identify concrete, purposeful action a careseeker would take in response to God's activity in the situation of need may specify elements of discipleship such as justice, healing, companionship, or, to use more spatial terms, recentering one's sense of place in the world. As stated earlier, faithfulness, resistance, and connection, the selected themes in this project, are not intended as a comprehensive picture of our activity in response to God but signal the importance of language in pastoral care that points toward the activity of God and suggests the responses we seek to foster.

The clearer caregivers become about our theological "location," the central assumptions about time and space that we bring to a process of care, the more likely it is that we will work in collaboration with careseekers to foster faithful response in the concrete, specific situation being addressed, without foreclosing new understanding and vision of what faithfulness may be. Whether we invite conversation about a person's sense of closeness to or distance from God, the person's sense of sacred space and place in God's creation, or engage in dialogue about a person's storied life in relation to the larger sacred history and future of God's activity and purpose, caregivers make crucial theological choices clarified and expanded by the contribution of feminist theologies.

In addition to the question of an adequate theology of God, a second issue in drawing from feminist theology as a source for pastoral care and counseling is the relation between human experience and our knowledge and interpretation of Jesus Christ. Although gender has not been the focus of this discussion, one aspect of attention to the historical Jesus concerns his "maleness."[51] I contend that it is Jesus' wholeness as both fully human and fully divine, not his maleness specifically, that enables him to be a savior for all people, a perspective shared by some other feminist and womanist theologians.[52] At the same time, Jesus Christ does have

---

51. I understand the term "gender" as a social construct that is shaped by a combination of sociocultural context, physiological capacities, and psychological structures. This definition is discussed in Rachel T. Hare-Mustin and Jeanne Marecek, eds., *Making a Difference: Psychology and the Construction of Gender* (New Haven: Yale University Press, 1990).

52. See especially Jacquelyn Grant, *White Women's Christ and Black Women's Jesus: Feminist Christology and Womanist Response* (Atlanta: Scholars Press, 1989), 220; and

the specificity and particularity of gender. Reconstructions of the historical Jesus sharpen the meaning of Jesus' gender as we imagine more of what "maleness" meant in his social and historical context and what faith interprets this to mean now. John Dominic Crossan's reconstruction of the historical Jesus, for instance, focuses on the unique intersection of material from cross-cultural anthropology, Greco-Roman and Jewish history, and literary and scriptural texts in relation to this "Mediterranean Jewish peasant."[53]

In Crossan's reconstruction, the lifestyle preached and embodied in Jesus' here-and-now kingdom of God contradicted the common values and practices of a male Jewish peasant of his day in several ways.[54] In the kingdom as proclaimed by Jesus, these values and practices occur not just in terms of personal or individual evil but as social, structural, or systemic injustice, which is, according to Crossan, precisely the imperial situation in which Jesus and his fellow peasants found themselves. Jesus contradicts the Mediterranean family's axis of power that separated one generation over against another, negating the potential abuse of power and commending an ideal family group in which power is equally accessible to all under God.

Political groupings are the reference in Crossan's interpretation of Jesus' blessing of the "poor," a blessing specific to the destitute, those who had nothing due to the operations of the political system. Interpreted in this way, all other political-economic classes of persons, even the poor who had enough to survive, bore responsibility for this "blessed" and innocent segment of society who would otherwise not survive. Crossan interprets the connection between little children and the kingdom of God in contrast to the meaning of infants in the Mediterranean world of pa-

---

Letty Russell, *Human Liberation in a Feminist Perspective: A Theology* (Philadelphia: Westminster Press, 1974), 136–37.

53. Crossan, *Jesus: A Revolutionary Biography,* xii. Claiming that Christianity always makes its best judgment about who Jesus was in the past, Crossan goes on from the basis of that reconstruction to decide what "Christ" means now. Crossan distinguishes between the historical Jesus and the Christ confessed in faith and clarifies the dialectic between the two: "Christian belief is (1) an act of faith (2) in the historical Jesus (3) as the manifestation of God." Ibid., 200.

54. Ibid., 54–74. Crossan critically assesses the term "kingdom of God" as a translation of the Greek word *basileia.* Crossan interprets this as the way in which power and rule are exercised, focusing on a process or way of life rather than a location on earth: "The Kingdom of God is people under divine rule and that, as ideal, transcends and judges all human rule.... The Kingdom of God is what the world would be if God were directly and immediately in charge" (55).

ternal power. Unless the father accepted the infant as a member of the family, he or she was abandoned to die or to be raised by someone else as a slave. The power and process proclaimed by Jesus takes the children up in his arms, lays hands on them, and blesses them, as a father would in accepting them into his family. Jesus also compared the kingdom to a mustard plant, which, in Crossan's analysis, is not just a plant that starts out small and grows into a large shrub but a plant that can take over where it is not wanted and destroy the garden or field.

A further example of what the kingdom of God meant for Jesus is what Crossan calls "open commensality," or eating together in a way that challenged the rules of association and socialization. Instead of reflecting the economic discrimination, social hierarchy, and political differentiation of the day, Jesus engaged in table fellowship with exactly those persons he would have avoided, had he followed the social rules. Crossan interprets this process of open commensality as a fundamental threat to the values of honor and shame based on social discrimination in ancient Mediterranean society. Crossan discusses the radical egalitarianism of Jesus' actions, carefully distinguishing it from contemporary democracy and suggesting that it is much more like a lottery than a democracy. In this way, Crossan locates Jesus' vision and work in "the ancient and universal peasant dream of a just and equal world."[55]

This brief summary of one perspective on aspects of the reconstructed historical Jesus offers support for a type of resistance that contradicts harmful social expectations and rules of behavior in favor of connections that heal and restore. Provided that it does not fully displace other reconstructions and theological interpretations, it may be appropriated into a broader theological understanding of Jesus Christ. As a source of knowledge contributing to pastoral care and counseling, this portrayal of Jesus may in turn alter our self-understanding and sense of relationship with the Christ of faith and change our notion of faithful response to God.[56]

---

55. Ibid., 74.

56. Criticizing symbols based on Jesus because they serve to justify suffering and victimization, some feminists contend that Jesus' maleness is an obstacle for women or that his suffering and obedience reinforce self-sacrifice in women. Francis Schüssler Fiorenza interprets these criticisms as ideological symbolization. He suggests that if one interprets the crucifixion and death of Jesus as the result of his life and work, "then one obtains a leverage point to place into check ideological symbolizations of Christ and to discover a resource for resistance. A major problem, leading to colonial and ideological use of Christian symbols, is precisely their dislocation from the historical concreteness of the life and praxis of Jesus." Fiorenza, "Christian Redemp-

The third issue in this summary of theological implications is theological anthropology and feminist contributions to a pastoral theological anthropology and adequate theory of self. Attention to the historical Jesus and the startling specificity of his actions in the sociocultural context of his day may prompt insight and alter action that results from pastoral care. God's liberative and reconciling activity is embodied in Jesus Christ through particular interactions that specify constructive opposition and unexpected inclusion, interactions that may resonate with dilemmas faced by careseekers. In this way, a more "performative" pastoral theology may emerge from feminist struggles with Christology that account for the specificity of the historical Jesus as well as the community that he called forth. Rather than abandoning the person Jesus Christ in favor of a focus on the community that emerged through him, a fuller Christology that appropriates some reconstruction of the historical Jesus seems to intensify the meaning of Jesus' engendered self. This fuller view of Jesus Christ portrays a new way for men and women to be in relationship, for economic injustice to be subverted, and for destructive use of power to be resisted. As Migliore points out in his discussion of liberation theology, "It is not our prior understandings of liberation that identify Jesus; rather, it is Jesus who incarnates and clarifies true liberation."[57] Knowledge of the historical concreteness of Jesus' life and work suggests that he was both shaped by that concreteness and free to act within it, interconnected with the context and choiceful in contradicting its requirements.

One implication for theological anthropology emerges from this view of Jesus' relation to the community that was formed through him. Mutual influence in the relationship of individual and community or context is possible without claiming absolute determinative power of one over the other. Further, the ambiguity of Jesus Christ as symbol is restored, affirming that divine transcendent power interpreted solely as over against humanity or creation is both insufficient and destructive and that heroic individual acts may be motivated by norms of an ideological community toward healing and justice. In other words, individual action or influence is not necessarily characterized by conformity in the negative sense, but may be self-expression, even inspired self-expression that also reflects the norms and values of an ideological community. To portray it otherwise loses sight of individual agency and the power to act, as if all individual ac-

tion between Colonialism and Pluralism," in *Reconstructing Christian Theology*, ed. Rebecca S. Chopp and Mark Lewis Taylor (Minneapolis: Fortress Press, 1994), 294.
57. Migliore, *Called to Freedom*, 45.

tion is merely compliance or as if a person does not remain an individual, even an individualist, while in healthy mutual relationship with others. If the restored meaning of the symbol encourages renewed attention to the constitutive influence of individual and community, this does have transformative possibilities that can be brought to bear on culture and on theology itself.

Pastoral theological anthropology is evident in caregiving when we discuss with careseekers the meaning and power of imago Dei and explore the significance of our "creatureliness." It is evident when we name sin in terms of systemic forces that perpetuate suffering, self-abnegation, and denial of agency, as well as in the more traditional language of idolatry and tyranny. Caregivers demonstrate their pastoral theological anthropology when we listen for and speak of health or wholeness, enhancing freedom, naming options, making commitments, and resolving problems and when we explicate the reason any of this is desirable and who is responsible for making it happen. Our participation in this process, the "performative" sense of pastoral theology, is demonstrated in part through ongoing discernment of what is faithful in a specific instance, what is an accurate and effective reflection of who we know God to be. As caregivers and careseekers work with the intrapsychic, interpersonal, and systemic dimensions of sin and appropriation of salvation, suffering and movement toward healing, brokenness and efforts toward coherence and wholeness, we revise our theology again and again as we learn more of how God is manifest.

A theology of God that acknowledges God's freedom and seeks to identify God's activity in intimate relation to the world may alter one's relationship with God, sense of personal or communal identity, and faithful response to God. Feminist theology and pastoral care will continue to exert mutual influence in emerging pastoral theological anthropology, which is altered in accounting for diverse collective and individual experiences and relationship with God. Feminist theology is moving beyond an exclusive focus on the experience of women, in part, because the experiences of oppression and difference it has addressed surely extend beyond gender categorization. As the voices of persons of color, the experiences of the poor and other marginalized groups, and the impact of our choices upon the environment become the focus of theological revisioning, these sources of knowledge will relativize previous assumptions and further alter our notions of faithful response to God.

Chapter Three

Feminist Psychotherapy as Theory of Change

Psychological theory offers an interpretation of how an individual's thoughts, feelings, and behavior are organized in intrapsychic structure and expressed and influenced in relationships embedded in culture. Psychotherapy is a process of change based upon a particular psychological interpretation or theory of self in which a person or group moves toward greater health or resolution of suffering as a result of relationship with a therapist or counselor. In this chapter, I use psychological interpretation and therapeutic process that emerges from psychotherapy as a supporting discipline for ministries of pastoral care and counseling, and I explore feminist theories of self and psychotherapy as specific interpretations of the self that commend change not only in individuals and families but in the social and cultural forces that influence them.

Following a summary of the issues involved in using this supporting discipline, I explore the psychological and therapeutic dimensions of careseekers' experiences, which were identified in the preceding chapter in theological terms as interconnection, resistance, and faithfulness. Thematizing the experience of persons I have encountered in pastoral ministries of care helps to identify patterns of need and the theology and theory of change that enhance response to that need. My intention in doing so is not to be comprehensive or to overdraw generalizations, but to suggest resonance among illustrative experiences of careseekers and selected theological and therapeutic sources of knowledge for pastoral care. I discuss the notion of difference and what makes healthy, interdependent connection possible, using a model of women's psychological development that values apparent differences in women's experiences as contrasted with men's experience.[1] I note how this interpretation may

---

1. I draw from Carol Gilligan, *In a Different Voice: Psychological Theory and Women's Development* (Cambridge: Harvard University Press, 1982); Carol Gilligan, Nona P. Lyons, and Trudy J. Hanmer, *Making Connections: The Relational Worlds of Adolescent Girls at Emma Willard School* (Cambridge: Harvard University Press, 1989); and

render variety within either gender less visible and, ironically, may focus attention away from changes needed in social and material conditions.

In the second part of the chapter, I argue for the necessity of resistance to harm and the relation of this action to supportive connections within a group, drawing from the feminist model of psychotherapy developed by Mary Ballou and Nancy Gabalac.[2] I discuss the hazards in an approach that may obscure commonalities among women and men as well as the limits of separation as a therapeutic goal. The third section focuses on a fuller theory of self that accounts for social and cultural influence but also identifies the dynamics of intrapsychic structure and interpersonal relations. I argue that coherence and congruity are integral to a theory of self and process of change for the purposes of pastoral care and counseling in promoting faithful relation to God, appropriate resistance to harm, and healthy, interdependent connections. The chapter concludes with discussion of the strengths and limits of an emphasis on oppression and difference and the paradoxes in utilizing feminist psychological and therapeutic theory.

Feminist psychological interpretation and therapeutic process of change are critical of the interstructuring of power as domination in relations with other persons and in social structures and institutions.[3] Caregivers seek to understand the manifestations of structured power and, with the larger community of faith, to participate in transforming the values, attitudes, and behaviors that result in misuse of power as domination. Many of the experiences that inform the feminist theories used in this chapter emerged from research with women in an effort to establish a more inclusive empirical base. In order to suggest that we

---

Carol Gilligan, Annie G. Rogers, and Deborah L. Tolman, eds., *Women, Girls, and Psychotherapy: Reframing Resistance* (New York: Haworth, 1991).

2. Mary Ballou and Nancy M. Gabalac, *A Feminist Position on Mental Health* (Springfield, Ill.: Charles C. Thomas, 1985).

3. A summary of the variety of feminist approaches within "feminist" therapy is offered in Laura S. Brown, *Subversive Dialogues: Theory in Feminist Therapy* (New York: Basic Books, 1994), 47–68. Brown identifies political, reformist, and radical interpretations in feminist therapy and notes the influence of postmodern and social-constructionist thought among some theorists in radical feminist therapy. She also provides a helpful discussion of the necessity of theorizing from diversity in feminist therapy, noting "it is critical that feminist therapists not assume the essentially gendered nature of phenomena that seem to be gender-linked but rather explore the potential plasticity and flexibility of these ways of being and examine the potential danger in assuming that characteristics are core to one's sense of self because of their presumed gender-linkage." Ibid., 68.

have much to learn through specifying experience regarding difference on the basis of gender and race, as well as other categories of experience not explored in this project, I note in particular research with African American women. In chapter 4, I will draw from the discussion of psychology and psychotherapy as supporting discipline to inform care, counseling, and consultation with women and men in individual, family, and congregation contexts and seek to maintain respect for the experience base that informed the development of these theories in the process.

Every pastoral caregiver and counselor has operative definitions of the self, of what it means to be a faithful person, and assumptions about the relation of health and faith. Evaluation of theories of self and therapeutic process as theory of change helps to surface these operative definitions and assumptions, opening them for critical reflection and revision. Pastoral care and counseling understand "health" not only in terms of psychological well-being but also with a specific theological view of the freedom and limits of human beings. This is a systemic perspective that analyzes a person's relationships with self, God, family, other social systems, and the environment.[4] Because I use psychological theories as a supporting discipline in this project, it is important to raise the question of what understandings of human being are assumed in these theories. This does not mean that the theories must be explicitly theological. However, how human freedom and limit are understood, how health is defined, how change is thought to occur, the type of relations intended as a result of change—these issues are important in discerning what psychological theories are appropriate for a theological endeavor.

One definition of feminist therapy is

> a practice of therapy informed by feminist political philosophy and analysis, grounded in multicultural feminist scholarship on the psychology of women and gender, which leads both therapist and client toward strategies and solutions advancing feminist resistance, transformation, and social change in daily personal life, and in relationships with the social, emotional, and political environment.[5]

---

4. Although I am not pursuing this discussion in terms of family systems theory, some family systems theorists have acknowledged the need for a fuller understanding of both self and system. See Michael P. Nichols, *The Self in the System* (New York: Brunner/Mazel, 1987); and Michael P. Nichols and Richard C. Schwartz, *Family Therapy: Concepts and Methods* (Boston: Allyn & Bacon, 1995), 60, and 148–50.

5. Brown, *Subversive Dialogues,* 22.

The distinguishing feature of a feminist practice of therapy is how the therapist thinks, rather than who the clients are, the techniques employed, or the problems addressed through therapy. A therapist's consciousness of the social and political context in which therapy occurs and the potential for distortion in the interpretation of experience due to that context is crucial in feminist therapy. Recognizing that a person's internal or intra-psychic experience is linked integrally with the external world and a specific social and political context informs the development of the ther-apeutic relationship, definition of problems, and goals of a process of change.

As interpretations of experience and strategies for action, feminist the-ories of self and change seek to increase freedom and possibility within structured relationships and may help to identify the distortions inter-nalized in the self and evident in the context. Feminist approaches that enhance freedom and acknowledge limits, that promote regard for differ-ence without inaccurately dichotomizing on the basis of gender, race, or other categories of experience, are more appropriate to the theo-logical concerns of pastoral care and counseling. Feminist practice of therapy may help caregivers identify healthy interconnections in com-munity viewed as one aspect of self, along with the distortions caused by the social and political context. Feminist theory offers caregivers an op-portunity to encourage individual initiative and action, to exert influence upon the problem, without losing sight of the influence of the prob-lem on the person. Rather than construing "individual" and "social" as opposite either in problem definition or resolution to suffering, a more accurate theological anthropology emerges through a feminist approach that accounts for social and culture influence but stops short of outright determinism, which would preclude individual agency and freedom.

Difference in Women's Psychology

Caregivers attend to difference in individuals and groups to whom they respond through active listening and clarification in order to be accu-rate and effective in the help they offer. Theological viewpoint, gender, race, sexual orientation, economic class, and a variety of other categories specify the diversity of experience caregivers encounter as they try to understand and adequately respond to problems careseekers encounter. The manner in which caregivers construe difference includes openness and flexibility in hearing from careseekers how their sense of self and the problem they currently face is connected to social and cultural influence.

Theorizing from diversity, as Laura Brown has pointed out, is a crucial aspect of feminist therapy and calls for a multicultural consciousness in addition to analysis of power as domination. Those of us who seek to offer care as a member of a "dominant" group must pay close attention to how our assumptions are played out in relation to persons we seek to help and how differences influence the dynamics of a helping relationship, the definition of a problem, and action toward its resolution.

Fostering faithfulness, appropriate resistance, or healthy, interdependent connections requires sufficient accounting for difference. The work of developmental psychologist Carol Gilligan and her colleagues suggests both clarity and ambiguity in the "difference" that difference makes, particularly as she discusses the themes of resistance and connection in relationships. The body of research Gilligan has pursued is no doubt limited and does not represent the wider multicultural and conceptually diverse base of scholarship that Brown commends for those practicing feminist therapy, but it may inform pastoral theological reflection on pastoral care as theory from a supporting discipline.

I have come to read Gilligan's work with caution because her challenge to developmental psychology, emphasizing collectivity as opposed to individuation and the establishment of an autonomous self, may be based on a misreading of Erik Erikson's thought.[6] Gilligan claims that Erikson's eight crises of development focus on "separateness" in such a way that "attachments appear to be developmental impediments."[7] However, a literalism in Gilligan's criticism of Erikson's terms "separateness" and "autonomy" is ironic and contradictory to her own use of the word "resistance" as desirable for development of the self. My purpose in using Gilligan's theory is to illustrate the possibilities and problems in emphasizing difference on the basis of gender and to analyze her work related to the themes of this project, but I do so with the understanding that the nuances of women's psychological development in Gilligan's work actually have their basis in a positive relation to (not in contradiction of) Erikson's theory. I would contend that Gilligan's work may be an exaggeration of difference with Erikson in particular and an exaggeration of gender difference more generally.

---

6. In conversation several years ago, Donald Capps pointed out a misrepresentation of Erikson's thought in Gilligan's work, in which she removes Erikson's stage theory from the corpus of his work. My brief discussion of Gilligan's misrepresentation is my understanding of the error.

7. Gilligan, *In a Different Voice*, 12–13.

Although I do not pursue the criticism of Gilligan's work related to Erikson's thought at length, a brief statement from Erikson's discussion of the second crisis of development—autonomy versus shame and doubt—illustrates the point. Erikson states that the social modalities of this second crisis are "holding on and letting go," each of which can lead to either hostile or benign expectations and attitudes:

> Outer control at this stage, therefore, must be firmly reassuring. The infant must come to feel that the basic faith in existence, which is the lasting treasure saved from the rages of the oral stage, will not be jeopardized by this about-face of his, this sudden violent wish to have a choice, to appropriate demandingly, and to eliminate stubbornly.
>
> Firmness must protect him against the potential anarchy of his as yet untrained sense of discrimination, his inability to hold on and to let go with discretion. As his environment encourages him to "stand on his own feet," it must protect him against meaningless and arbitrary experiences of shame and of early doubt.[8]

Gilligan's work is an effort to correct an emphasis on separation or a requirement to break emotional ties in relationship for the sake of autonomy and development, but it is based on a false premise that differentiation occurs through separation from relationship. It is important to explore what happens as a result of this misrepresentation for the purposes of this project.

In their research, Gilligan and her colleagues elaborate the themes of resistance and connection as they explore psychological development in adolescent girls. I summarize these themes as they find expression in their research and take into consideration the critical perspective of African American contributors in Gilligan's project. Commenting in the introduction to their text, the editors describe the strength of resistance to psychotherapy often found in adolescent girls:

> We elaborate the concept of resistance by joining girls' struggle to know what they know and speak about their thoughts and feelings. In doing so we acknowledge the difficulty girls face when their knowledge or feelings seem hurtful to other people or disruptive of relationships. Thus the word resistance takes on new resonances, picking up the notion of healthy resistance, the capacity of the psyche to resist disease processes, and also the concept of political resistance, the willingness to act on one's own knowledge when such action creates trouble. In reframing resistance as a psychological strength, as potentially healthy and a mark of courage, we

---

8. Erik Erikson, *Childhood and Society,* 2d ed. (New York: W. W. Norton, 1963), 251–52.

draw on the data of our research which shows that girls' psychological health in adolescence, like the psychological health of women, depends on their resistance to inauthentic or false relationships.[9]

In her own essay in the collection, Gilligan gives a colorful portrayal of the ten girls who participated in a research group over a period of two years. In her detailed description of their interactions, Gilligan explains the meaning of false relationships, as the girls turn their faces and voices into those "nice, smiling and interested" girls. She describes the girls' imitation of the high-pitched breathiness of "the too-good-to-be-true woman" in which voice is used "to cover rather than to convey thoughts and feelings" and thus "to close rather than to open a channel of connection between people."[10] As the girls proceeded with their imitations of women's greeting rituals and social gestures, Gilligan perceives the capacity to separate voice from actual feelings and thoughts. She contrasts the facility for imitation and false relationship in ten- and eleven-year-olds with the relational honesty of seven- and eight-year-old girls, who talk about what is happening in relationships even if it is painful or risky to do so. Gilligan concludes that the older girls learn to "silence their relational knowledge," in effect taking themselves out of honest relationship for the sake of maintaining a relationship, albeit a false one. However, one could make the counterargument that relational knowledge makes possible the type of imitation or social learning Gilligan describes. If this is accurate, sacrifice of relational knowing is not so much the issue as sufficient op-

---

9. Gilligan, Rogers, and Tolman, eds., *Women, Girls, and Psychotherapy*, 1–2. I will discuss later in this chapter how Gilligan explores resistance as a psychological strength and a mark of courage but fails to explore fully the ambiguity of resistance, which, although a sign of vitality, may be incongruent or inappropriate to the situation. I suggest that a more complete understanding of resistance must be developed.

10. Gilligan's research has been criticized for lack of attention to issues of race and class. See especially Judith Stacey, "On Resistance, Ambivalence, and Feminist Theory: A Response to Carol Gilligan," *Michigan Quarterly Review* (1991): 537–46. Stacey commends Gilligan for locating "resistance," as a liberatory capacity, in the very same desire for relationship that leads girls to falseness in relationship. However, Stacey is quite critical of Gilligan (and other standpoint feminist theorists such as Nancy Hartsock, Sandra Harding, and Sara Ruddick) for being overconfident in their feminist humanism and for continuing to use uncritically universalist gender categories. Standing more with postmodern feminist theorists who use deconstructionist modes of thought to celebrate diversity and acknowledge limitations of any perspective, Stacey offers a cogent analysis of one of Gilligan's vignettes using social class, rather than gender, as a basis for explaining an adolescent girl's behavior.

portunity for relationship with more mature and "authentic" adults, an issue for both boys and girls.

Gilligan's hypothesis is that adolescence for girls is comparable to early childhood for boys in that both enter a relational crisis in which, for the sake of relationship, one takes oneself out of relationship.[11] Gilligan suggests Freud's notion of the Oedipus complex as the most profound relational crisis for boys as they move toward identification with the father. She argues that the struggle for girls and boys is primarily one of staying in relationship and that the resistance to disconnection is healthy. The resistance is to loss—for boys, giving up identification with or idealization of the mother, and for girls, giving up the reality of honest relationships to take on the image of perfection as "the model of the pure or perfectly good woman." Healthy resistance to loss and disconnection becomes a political struggle, according to Gilligan, as pressure is brought to bear on behalf of the "prevailing order of social relationships." What has become a political struggle in the context of prevailing social order then becomes a psychological struggle or resistance to loss of connection and relationship. Gilligan questions the necessity for what she considers the central paradox of psychological development for both women and men—taking oneself out of relationship for the sake of relationships.[12]

In Gilligan's volume, two essays reflecting the experiences of African American women offer an alternative view of resistance and connection. Beverly Jean Smith states that her relationship with her own mother equipped her to resist others' definitional norms.[13] She describes the "call

---

11. Gilligan, "Women's Psychological Development: Implications for Psychotherapy," in *Women, Girls, and Psychotherapy,* ed. Gilligan, Rogers, and Tolman, 16.

12. Ibid., 23. In her development of a new psychology of women, Ellyn Kaschak critiques the branch of feminist psychological thought developed by feminist object relations theorists identified as Carol Gilligan, Jean Baker Miller, Nancy Chodorow, and Dorothy Dinnerstein. Kaschak views the principles of object relations theory as reductionist for purposes of gender analysis and recommends developing a qualitatively different feminist paradigm. In her view, a notable hazard among feminist object relations theorists is the promotion of a female relational style as psychologically superior and preferable for the needs of humanity. Kaschak views this perspective as perpetuating a post-Cartesian construct of "separate dichotomous gender categories and decontextualized universal attributes." She contends that this perspective separates human qualities and choices from the larger social context. Ellyn Kaschak, *Engendered Lives: A New Psychology of Women's Experience* (New York: Basic Books, 1992), 27.

13. Beverly Jean Smith, "Raising a Resister," in *Women, Girls, and Psychotherapy,* ed. Gilligan, Rogers, and Tolman, 137–48.

and response" in African American culture as valuing voice and the capacity to speak up and say what you think. This was balanced with a demand that individual voices be connected to the whole and "not just to go solo and fly off somewhere":

> A group of my female friends and I met. A conversation begins. Before we know it, all of us are speaking at the same time on the subject that has been raised by someone. Somehow, one voice gets the lead, while the rest of us become the background music. Eventually, another voice rises to displace the previous lead voice that joins us in the background.... A connectedness exists for African Americans between the individual and those around her or him, in all of these scenes. From birth, I feel I have understood the triadic concept of the individual, the family, and the universe.[14]

Smith states that homemaking and child rearing were valued in the black community where she grew up, and in addition to these tasks, almost all the women worked outside the home. She describes black women as the "forerunners of what later white feminists wanted to become: independent, working, jugglers of self and family."[15] However, Smith does not discuss the conditions (intrapsychic, personal, or social) under which a person needs to accept and learn from definitional norms outside the family or identifying group. For example, in families where self-definition and differentiation of self are discouraged, one must often form attachments outside the family in order to achieve sufficient autonomy for authentic self-expression. The same sort of dynamic may occur in ideological groupings in which individuality and diversity are not well tolerated and not encouraged as enhancing creative possibility.

In another essay in the same volume, Tracy Robinson and Janie Ward, African American educational and developmental psychologists, draw upon their experience as women and scholars to distinguish between resistance for survival and resistance for liberation.[16] Forms of resistance for survival may be dysfunctional adaptations to an oppressive reality that offer only short-term relief. These strategies of resistance are potentially destructive elements in the sociocultural environment of young African American women and include "self-denigration due to the internalization of negative self images, excessive autonomy and individualism at the

---

14. Ibid., 140–41.
15. Ibid., 143.
16. Tracy Robinson and Janie Victoria Ward, "A Belief in Self Far Greater than Anyone's Disbelief: Cultivating Resistance among African American Female Adolescents," in *Women, Girls, and Psychotherapy,* ed. Gilligan, Rogers, and Tolman, 87–103.

expense of connectedness to the collective,... and 'quick fixes' such as early and unplanned pregnancies, substance abuse, school failure and food addictions."[17] Forms of resistance for liberation, on the other hand, are strategies in which black girls and women "are encouraged to acknowledge the problems of, and to demand change in, an environment that oppresses them."[18]

Robinson and Ward offer four types of resistance for liberation. The first is resistance to negative images of the self by confronting and rejecting negative evaluations of blackness and femaleness and by embracing the admirable qualities of black womanhood. The second is resistance to excessive individualism, which they understand to be a "EuroAmerican principle" rooted in Erikson's developmental psychology in which one is encouraged to achieve autonomy by breaking away from others, thus discovering oneself. However, this criticism again signals a misinterpretation of Erikson's thought and a kind of literalism in understanding the word "separation," removing it from Erikson's context of developmental challenges for the self. Robinson and Ward point out the "extended" definition of the self as "we" in an African worldview and the recognition of the individual's connectedness with others in this understanding of "extended self."

Robinson and Ward cite the work of Gilligan and of Jean Baker Miller on connections and interdependence in the psychological development of women as further support for this particular attunement in African American women.[19] They decry "racelessness," which they understand as the desire to minimize cultural connections, and view this as a disturbing strategy among some high-achieving black students. The authors support individual effort but also argue that a value orientation, which promotes only individual fulfillment, may be detrimental to the collective African American identity:

> The importance of hard work and communalism is viewed threefold: as a personal responsibility, as an intergenerational commitment to family, and as a tie to the larger collective. A resistant strategy of liberation, in keeping with African American traditional values, ties individual achievement

---

17. Ibid., 89.

18. Ibid. The authors cite the work of L. Fulanie, ed., *The Psychopathology of Racism and Sexism* (New York: Harrington Park Press, 1988), as particularly helpful in promoting a therapy of empowerment that encourages these strategies of resistance for liberation.

19. Robinson and Ward cite Gilligan, *In a Different Voice*; and Jean Baker Miller, *Toward a New Psychology of Women* (Boston: Beacon Press, 1976).

to collective struggle. In the service of personal and cultural liberation, African American adolescent girls must resist an individualism that sees the self as disconnected from others in the black community and, as it is culturally and psychologically dysfunctional, she must resist those who might advocate her isolation and separation from traditional African American cultural practices, values and beliefs.[20]

The second form of resistance for liberation commends, then, an "extended self" that affirms connections within African American cultural practices as an alternative to "excessive individualism." The third form of resistance is to avoid quick fixes, which are self-destructive behaviors with disempowering consequences. As the fourth form of resistance, Robinson and Ward recommend adopting an "Afrocentric" model that includes gender-specific concerns and an Afrocentric perspective on racial identity.[21]

In specific suggestions for the clinical community, the authors recommend that therapists assess whether clients are engaged in resistance for survival or for liberation. This involves asking whether a survival strategy is actually self-destructive or if resistance has both self-affirmation and community validation as its goals.[22] Therapists are encouraged to relabel behavior as resistance, which can then be channeled in liberative forms:

> Thus relabelling to foster healthy resistance serves three purposes: first, it aids in establishing an empathic and supportive therapeutic relationship; second, it enables the clinician to affirm behaviors and attitudes positively that had been mislabeled and misunderstood previously; and third, the relabelling process helps the client to take responsibility for negative behaviors that are self-denigrating and, through critical analysis and con-

---

20. Robinson and Ward, "A Belief in Self," 94.

21. It would be possible to argue for self-definition within community on the basis of Erikson's thought, as for instance in his analysis of Native American populations in which the ego is understood as the interdependence of inner and social organization. See Erikson, *Childhood and Society,* 114–86.

22. Robinson and Ward, "A Belief in Self," 98. The authors develop the notion of an Afrocentric worldview based on an awareness of African culture and traditions. In order to foster resistance for liberation and empowerment among African American adolescent girls, they identify an African value system called Nguzo Saba, a value system that African Americans are encouraged to adopt. The authors cite M. Karenga, *Kawaida Theory* (Los Angeles: Kawaida, 1980), as their source. Based on traditional African philosophies, the seven principles of the Nguzo Saba are *umoja* (unity), *kujichagulia* (self-determination), *ujima* (collective work and responsibility), *ujaama* (cooperative economics), *nia* (purpose), *kuumba* (creativity), and *imani* (faith).

frontation, begin to make changes that are self-affirming and conducive to positive psychological development.[23]

The essays by African American women psychologists offer alternative perspectives on the themes of connection and resistance from a psychological framework, which are suggestive of what faithfulness might mean if diversity is assumed to be the rule rather than the exception in pastoral care. Portraying her own socialization as feeling connected while acting alone, Smith views connectedness and independence as not mutually exclusive. In fact, as she describes it, her closest connections with family are the very relationships in which she learned to think for herself and about herself in an affirming way.

Robinson and Ward's essay portrays the racist context in which African American adolescent girls choose forms of resistance, distinguishing the liberative forms as those that promote the "liberation of one's self and one's community" and that draw upon "the strengths of one's history and cultural connections."[24] They offer strategies for liberation that are specifically grounded in African philosophies and suggest that in order to cultivate healthy resistance clinicians should relabel behaviors that occur in a hostile sociopolitical climate.

One implication for pastoral theological reflection on practice of ministry may be the influence of the group or community with which the person most identifies and the manner in which participation in it nurtures coherent sense of self and enhances freedom to express oneself, tolerating or even celebrating diversity. For instance, I have discussed faithfulness in response to God as not only an individual and communal issue but as a part of the context of pastoral care and counseling. However, people may or may not hold relation to God or practice of faith as primary elements of self-identification, and engagement in multiple groups or identifying with more than one community presents a challenge for maintaining coherence in identity and purpose. Separation from a group or system with which one has been connected may also be an effective strategy and, in some instances, even named as a step of faith.

Separation from Harm and Oppression

Pastoral care and counseling carry implicit assumptions about health and its relation to faithfulness in response to God. Feminist therapeutic theory

23. Ibid., 101.
24. Ibid., 90.

helps caregivers become more explicit about these assumptions and identifies a process of change through which greater health may be achieved. The model explored in this section specifies challenges to mental health in women's experience and raises several questions about how caregivers may effectively participate in a process of healing when dynamics of power are taken into account. In their statement on mental health, Ballou and Gabalac offer a framework for the complex issue of health, identifying shared principles regarding a feminist view of mental health.[25] The principles are a reliance on and validation of women's experience, recognition of the tremendous diversity of women's experiences with a responsibility for decreasing one's ethnocentrism, acknowledgment of relationships among all who have *not* shaped the dominant values in U.S. mental health theory and practice, and commitment to changing structures and processes in order to discover women's "unoppressed" nature.[26]

Two key terms in this position statement are "power systems" and "mental health." *Power systems* are organized groups and structures that have culturally approved legitimized status, with reward given only to those who conform to these dominant patterns of social and economic organization.[27] Distinguishing *mental health* from the medical model, which defines it as absence of pathology, Ballou and Gabalac identify what would constitute healthy relationships to other people, society, and the environment. They do not view mental health as adjustment to social norms nor locate it only within the individual, as in existential, Gestalt, and self theory, because to do so neglects analysis of the impact of social forces on women.

Acknowledging that a feminist conception of mental health has not yet been achieved, Ballou and Gabalac identify "constructs" of mental health intended as participation in the process of developing a feminist theory of mental health. Their constructs describe a healthy woman paraphrased in the following terms:

- experiencing herself as a woman, including both devaluation and valuation of this aspect of her identity;

- receiving data from herself, others, and the environment without distorting her perceptual process;

---

25. Ballou and Gabalac, *A Feminist Position on Mental Health*.
26. Ibid., 59–60.
27. Ibid., 71–72.

- processing data, even when it is contaminated and must be decoded for its valid meaning, and increasingly using her own experience and analyses as the central criterion;

- making decisions based on her processing of data, decisions that promote survival and growth for herself in positive relationships with others and with the environment;

- making judgments about needs, goals, and consequences of her behavior;

- being aware of and using her power;

- demonstrating knowledge about herself as she acts on her commitments;

- challenging and changing what can be changed in herself and society based on her commitments and analyses;

- learning to survive what cannot be changed.[28]

A healthy woman is capable of engaging the contradictions between victimization and agency and is able to negotiate both social constraints and individual responsibility.[29] The model views gender as one basis for oppression and promotes attention to the constrained roles and options experienced by women as critical and causative factors that must be given central consideration in responding to their mental health problems. The social analysis of the power-system environment and its contribution to feelings of self-hate and hopelessness is a key factor in the process of healing.

Affirming human agency in the midst of limiting or damaging circumstances and encouraging persons to change what can be changed are important contributions of this model. Identifying what can be changed involves analysis of harmful adaptation as a process of accommodating dominant, patriarchal culture. Adaptation may extend over a lifetime and damage women's health as they learn to deny the validity of their feelings and perceptions and to conform to roles defined by the larger systems of power in which they live, including family, social institutions, and larger sociopolitical systems. The factors that make it particularly difficult for women to achieve or maintain mental health include retribution for not complying with the norms of behavior or appearance prescribed for women, since power systems reward only those who conform. The message of retribution is that to resist inculcation

> is to go against the will of all the powers that be, to flaunt one's claim of equality before God, Man and Nature, thus bringing down upon one's

---

28. Ibid., 76.
29. Ibid., 76–77.

head the just punishments of the deity, society and biology. . . . Retribution reminds women that submission can be forced upon them. It prepares them through fear, escalated to the point of exhaustion and resignation, to deny themselves the option of resisting the application of their inculcation learnings to their lives.[30]

Adaptation includes the socialization and internalization that result in self-negating, self-destructive learning from the cultural context. Of particular interest in Ballou and Gabalac's analysis of this process is the use of several religious terms, such as conversion, salvation, and faith, and identification of God with "the powers that be." They understand *conversion* as denying responsibility for oneself and entrusting care of oneself to someone else's strength and *salvation* as that peace of mind gained through using one's inferior status in a life of service to others. A part of the "convert's" belief and faith in the process of harmful adaptation to inferior status as a woman is recruiting other women into accepting dependent relationships:

> The convert's belief is an effective coping mechanism for the fear, guilt and anxiety generated by the double bind of retribution. If, however, her new faith is all that holds together a broken spirit, a self-hating person concealed within a saint's demeanor, her own feelings of helplessness may show in the rigidity of her thinking, the self-righteousness of her defense of her behavior, and the desperation of her need to have others agree with her.[31]

The contradictions in the lives of women who are either unwilling or unable to be "converted" to harmful adaptation are evident in the lack of congruence between (1) the woman's feelings and experiences and (2) the power system in which she lives. The pain of these contradictions, her unhappiness as an "unbeliever," and her inability to continue in a role of selfless servant may lead her to seek help. If the woman does seek therapy, she may experience further harm from the mental health community. But if feminist therapy is practiced, she begins a process of corrective action and health maintenance.

These two elements in the therapeutic process may help the woman to validate and trust her thoughts and perceptions. Corrective action and health maintenance are simultaneous and parallel in the process, with corrective action focusing on developing the woman's sense of her own agency. Separation from oppressive systems is an element in this action and entails development of an alternative, positive concept of self and a critical view of the bias of the harmful systems to which she has adapted.

---

30. Ibid., 90.
31. Ibid., 94.

Corrective action includes recognizing her own feelings and thoughts and beginning to negotiate with existing power systems to meet her own goals, including "active resistance to harm" in interaction with these systems and withdrawal for purposes of self-protection, if necessary.

The Ballou and Gabalac model of feminist therapy may be compared with Gilligan's analysis of psychological development in their respective emphases on separating from power systems and refusing harmful adaptation, as distinguished from a focus on women's social and relational capacities, in terms of resisting disconnection on behalf of a more authentic self. Gilligan suggests that adapting or changing oneself to fit a particular circumstance or respond to another is a valued relational capacity provided one has a sufficiently formed sense of self.[32] Ballou and Gabalac argue that a particular type of adaptation is harmful when understood in a wider sociocultural context because it results in self-negating thoughts and behavior. Their model clarifies how such adaptation creates a painful challenge in which the self must separate from harmful influence in order to achieve a differentiated self more capable of healthy relationship. The theoretical difference rests on whether the adaptation of self to other or to a power system enhances the self, its freedom and coherence, rather than results in self-negation or fragmentation. It may be quite difficult to discern, except in retrospect, whether or not adaptation to another person or group is desirable, particularly if it appears to meet the individual's needs. Developing a notion of resistance as a theological, political, and psychological term enhances the possibility of creative resistance that is appropriate to a situation's potential for harm.

Corrective action, as interpreted by Ballou and Gabalac, occurs through individual and group therapy in which one gains enough distance from harmful forces to be able to see and name them and, in a supportive context, begin to hope for and implement alternative ways of living. The careseeker

---

32. A similar point is made in the Stone Center project, in which women's capacity for empathy with another person's inner thoughts and feelings is analyzed on the basis of a special mother-daughter bond in a child's infancy. The Stone Center authors draw upon Heinz Kohut's understanding of empathy in order to develop their analysis, but they do not address the contradictions in their reliance upon and critique of Kohut's work. The full name of the center is the Robert S. and Grace W. Stone Center for Developmental Services and Studies, Wellesley College, Wellesley, MA 02181. Since 1981 the center has developed research programs in psychological development and the prevention of psychological distress. See Judith V. Jordan et al., eds., *Women's Growth in Connection: Writings from the Stone Center* (New York: Guilford Press, 1991), 2.

gains critical awareness of the effects of political and economic systems and gains perspective on how the diversity and capability of women could be better supported and on how attitudes that increase the likelihood of violence against women could be contradicted. Corrective action in this model of feminist therapy involves unlearning internalized assumptions and resulting behaviors and beginning to trust self-affirming, "woman-affirming" attitudes. Variation in the degree of harmful adaptation and dependent attitudes and behaviors in the woman seeking help affects the difficulty of this separation process. For some women, it may be very frightening and painful as the therapist assists her in beginning to heal herself. The separation that occurs is largely cognitive, altering assumptions and perceptions, but "corrective action" may involve change in other behavior as well. The emotions experienced in this process of separation, especially anger, are validated, as assumptions about trusted people and institutions are examined. In feminist therapy, feelings are considered to be as political as thoughts and actions, and there are both empathic responses and caring confrontations.

The model's emphasis on the harmful influence of social and cultural forces offers an important alternative to therapeutic models that focus almost exclusively on intrapsychic or interpersonal processes. At the same time, we must acknowledge the ambiguity in identifying harmful power systems and cultural influences so that "harmful" is attributed with discernment. Many of us, at one time or another, reflect a dominant power system from which someone may need to separate on behalf of health. Caregivers who function as representatives of a faith tradition may experience such separation as rejection if it is overpersonalized; still situations may arise in which a person refuses the care we offer on the basis of our participation in a faith tradition "power system" perceived as harmful, regardless of our careful use of power or empowering intentions. Others may experience some risk in developing a relationship of trust with a caregiver but, having done so, may see that the "living" faith tradition in a local congregation, for example, includes instances of "limited" harm that are addressed and structured relations of power that seem to work well enough, and so they persist in the life of the faith community.

Health maintenance is interwoven with corrective action and focuses on experiences of collaboration and community building with other women for the purpose of strategizing to change the power systems that have devalued them. The second element of this model of feminist therapy may occur in study or support groups, groups focused on political action, or any group of women that does not perpetuate adaptation to harmful cultural stereotypes. A maintenance phase in therapy implies a realistic assessment of the kind of ongoing work required for women to continue working for change and remaining healthy. A place set apart from harmful cultural influences provides space where women can sustain realistic hope for change and develop strategies for change:

> The preparation for the confrontation of power system sexism is the building of community among women who are self-confident and aware of the elements in society hostile to them. Feminist therapists need to be active members of the health maintenance community for several reasons: to safeguard their own health, rights and opportunities; to demonstrate egalitarian working relationships for their clients; and to live out the principles of feminism, devoting a part of their lives toward the improved status of all women.[33]

The experience of community with women is a prerequisite for women's health in this therapeutic theory of change. The authors acknowledge that their experience with feminist egalitarian social structures that support women's health is limited and that we can only imagine such structures. In existence is a wide variety of support groups, some of which may provide a safe space to sustain women's mental health. One problem with the model's notion of developing a concept of self apart from power systems is its failure to address adequately the problem of the community or group in which this self-understanding is formed. People join groups for many reasons, including personal and political ones, and we must understand resistance as both. In a positive sense, this would suggest that a personal rationale for joining a women's growth group, for instance, may be a desire for support, an interest in hearing other women's stories, and the enjoyment of being with other women. But if one's reasons for joining a group are political and psychological as well, we need a more adequate understanding of the inner self in order to understand how a group may be beneficial as well as to insure that participation does not obscure some other meaning that requires critical awareness.

Experience of oppression or exploitation may be a basis for unity and a reason for joining a group, but this identity may obscure a woman's sense of her own agency and power, the ways in which she oppresses or misuses power, or the unclaimed opportunities she has to exercise power. A theory of self that takes into account the human tendency to resist even beneficial, consciously desired changes must be used. The Ballou and Gabalac model seems to suggest that a woman can reclaim thoughts and feelings

---

33. Ballou and Gabalac, *A Feminist Position on Mental Health*, 120.

that are incongruent with power systems that have influenced her but does not analyze the group or community of women with whom she is now identifying as a power system itself. The hazard would be in merely shifting dependency to a new system or overidentifying with a group in which the diversity of views may have been sacrificed for the sake of unity. One can gain much through cognitive awareness of and separation from harmful influence, but it is unlikely that the issues involved are only cognitive. For this reason, psychological theory that more clearly accounts for the structure and dynamics of the inner self is necessary.

An additional problem with the Ballou and Gabalac model is its failure to address interdependence with men and to acknowledge that men may participate in and support a woman's consciousness of harm and corrective action for the sake of health. Although the strength of the model is its insistence upon cognitive separation from harm in the context of community with women, for some women this occurs with both women and men. If separation from harmful aspects of culture is possible for women, it is possible for men as well, and women and men then actively support these processes for enhancing mental health for all persons.

References to God and church authority in this model of feminist therapy assume that God is one of the powers from which a woman must separate herself in order to move toward health.[34] The model, as a theory of psychotherapy, does not take into account the possibility of a sense of dependence on God as a healthy attribute or a relationship with God calling forth the courage and freedom she seeks. One of the contributions pastoral theology can make to the discipline of feminist therapy is the possibility of relationship with God and participation in ministries of the church contributing to women's health. Some pastoral caregivers and counselors do analyze sex roles and power differences in relationship to facilitate women's health. Encouraging critical consciousness in women and men allows new possibilities for relationship with and faithful response to God, confirming the history of both empowerment and exploitation in the church. As a representative of "church authorities," a pastoral counselor is in a particularly powerful position to promote harm or good among clients whose thoughts and feelings about the church do not conform to those of their own church authorities. It is possible for a representative of the church to promote critical awareness of the ambiguity of power as it is structured in the church, to invite conversation

---

34. Ibid., 90.

about God's power and activity and about the "is and is not" quality of language, symbols, and representatives in the community of faith.

Continuity and Self Psychology

Achieving freedom from harmful structures of power through cognitive separation is one perspective on how change can occur through a feminist approach in therapy. In the context of patriarchal society, a self is connected through political, social, and internalized arrangements of power and possibilities of freedom and responsibility. Understanding how people are able to resist harm, separate from sources of harm, and function autonomously enough to protect themselves, while maintaining healthy connections with other persons and systems, requires a broader theory of self. Pastoral care and counseling will be more likely to foster faithful response to God, appropriate resistance to harm, and healthy interdependent connections when informed by psychological and therapeutic theories that identify desirable congruity of the self as well as necessary change. As it is used here, *congruity* does not mean that a person remains exactly the same but suggests a recognizable correspondence and "fit" in one's sense of identity and patterns of behavior over time and place. Before discussing the contribution of self psychology to a broader theory of self, I offer this brief exploration of congruity as it relates to resistance to illustrate the point.

Resistance—in both the political and the psychological sense—can be a sign of vitality and resourcefulness that is connected and relevant to the desired healing or change.[35] James E. Dittes has suggested that resistance is, never automatic or accidental, but purposeful and motivated, a kind of "acted-out rationalization" based on inner promptings and "objective reality." Dittes claims that some unwelcome obstructive behavior encountered in a local church is a meaningful reaction. In the pastoral consultation vignette, for example, some members of the board at First Community Church persist in efforts to re-create the past in what appears to be resistance to inevitable change. Others venture forth into the future with a conviction that their vision is morally superior. The former resistance may be interpreted as obstructive behavior congruent with unarticulated meanings in the inner self, meanings that become much more ambiguous in public expression. The latter conviction may be con-

---

35. This idea is suggested in James E. Dittes, *The Church in the Way* (New York: Scribner, 1967), 136–85.

gruent with more public knowledge but fails to consider the vitality and endurance of personal meanings associated with the congregation's life.

Dittes discusses Adam and Eve as venturing out of childlike innocence into some assumption of responsibility, decision, and selfhood, 'an adventure that turned out ambiguously. Their resistance was occasioned by "risk-filled exercise of human freedom and responsibility," which he views as daring steps toward fuller selfhood.

> Resistance is an active, vigorous response by a sensitive person to significant confrontation. Further, it reveals a commitment to remain inside the given situation however conflicted and problematic, and to address it in its own terms. Resistance does not accidentally or passively just happen. It is prompted, and behind this prompting is a vital sensitivity and responsiveness.[36]

From this viewpoint, political resistance in a feminist perspective has one basis in the need for change in conditions and circumstances of material reality, and that resistance will be shaped by the particular demands for change in a specific situation or circumstance. But it also suggests that the political is personal and psychological, in the sense of having another basis in "inner promptings" with which the forms of resistance also have certain congruence. As Dittes points out, the "gap in congruence" with actual facts, or ambiguity in the form of resistance, becomes the evidence that inner meaning is also present in the rationalization. As a person becomes conscious of harmful adaptation, it is necessary to maintain some sense of the possible "gap in congruence" where the analysis of harm may be partially accurate but also distorted by the influence of the inner self.

I argue that awareness of a gap or incongruence between the situation and our response to it can result in a more appropriate, effective, and creative response that accurately "fits" the problem and thus helps to change both the situation and ourselves. The Ballou and Gabalac model is quite helpful in directing attention to harmful influences and becoming conscious of them in order to form a healthier resistive response. In addition, I am suggesting that self-critical awareness of internal influences and expressions of inner self prevents forms of resistance that are too partial or inappropriate, or that only serve purposes of retribution, and enables more creative, effective forms of resistance to be identified and carried forth. Kohut's theory of the nuclear, bipolar self demonstrates the possibility of a more complete theory of self, identifying dynamics

---

36. Ibid., 138.

of intrapsychic structure and interpersonal relations that make appropriate resistance, interdependent connections, and regard for difference more
possible.[37] His work gives a particular perspective on enhancing human
freedom and integrity that does not ignore gender difference but establishes a sense of the specificity and individuality of our self-structure and
self-expression. At the same time, because he understands the context
of the self as a narcissistic culture in which the individual struggles for
coherence and integrity, there is a sense of our commonality and shared
humanity interwoven with our particularity. Kohut establishes his theory
of a nuclear, bipolar self as a "reconstruction" on the basis of observations
in a therapeutic setting.

Kohut distinguishes himself from traditional psychoanalysis and object relations theorists in identifying his work as "self psychology." He
assesses the ongoing evolution of narcissistic issues in an individual's life
in addition to, "not in contradiction of," the more familiar resolutions of
oedipal conflict in psychoanalytic perspective that occur at various points
in development. Kohut posits a function of narcissism as contributing to
a person's health and adaptation, as it is transformed in the structure of
the "bipolar self."[38] *Primary narcissism* is the original experience of the in-

---

37. Heinz Kohut, *How Does Analysis Cure?* (Chicago: University of Chicago Press,
1984); and *The Restoration of the Self* (Madison, Conn.: International Universities
Press, 1977). Because Kohut's emphasis is not primarily upon oedipal conflicts, his
theory of the internal self is more amenable to the purposes of this project than
other object relations theory or psychoanalytic approaches that seem to move gender difference into opposition. Kohut states that in "patriarchally organized groups"
parental attitudes may foster mental structure characterized by "a firm superego and a
set of strong masculine ideas." He goes on to suggest that parental attitudes in which
gender differentiation has lessened "may produce, in consequence of different responses to the oedipal child, girls whose superego firmness and ideals correspond
more to that normally found in boys of the patriarchal group. And such girls may
well be specifically adapted to the tasks of a society that is nonexpansive—perhaps
the societies of the stabilized populations of tomorrow." *Restoration of the Self*, 232.
My brief overview of Kohut's theory of personality is drawn primarily from this text.

Family systems theorists Nichols and Schwartz note that Kohut has had a revo-
lutionizing impact on the psychoanalytic world and, indirectly, on family therapy:
"Kohut replaced Freud's raging id with an insecure self at the core of human nature
and taught us that our lives are organized around a striving for fulfillment and longing
for acceptance, more than around sex and aggression." *Family Therapy*, 149.

38. Kohut, *Restoration of the Self*, 171–219. Based on his clinical work, Kohut
carefully distinguishes psychopathology in primary self-disturbances (narcissistic personality disorder and narcissistic behavior disorders) from the narcissistic needs of the
personality and its ambitions, which may be used in a healthy and adaptive man-

fant in relation to the mother when the infant has not yet differentiated between self and other and when all "objects" in the environment, including the mother, are "self-objects." According to Kohut, it is through the responses to needs and the affirmative "mirroring" of the mother that the "nuclear self" of the infant is established. The formation of the "narcissistic self" with grandiose and exhibitionistic qualities occurs when grandiosity consolidates into ambitions in early childhood. These early constituents of the self, according to Kohut, are derived primarily from the relation with the maternal self-object as she mirrors acceptance and confirms grandiosity. (This is not the same as the ego ideal that controls drives in the psychic economy but is rather interwoven with the drives and "channels" them.)

When the primary narcissism is disturbed by the inevitable delays in responding to the infant's needs, the first narcissistic injury occurs, which causes changes in the psychic structure with formation of an "idealized parent imago" in an attempt to maintain the self's original perfection and omnipotence. Kohut maintains that the idealized goal structures are acquired in later childhood and may relate to parental figures of either sex. The image of the idealized parent is invested with libidinal energy and is thought to change as the child matures cognitively and with environmental influences, manifested in the person's goals and ideals.[39]

According to Kohut's theory, the tension between these two poles of the self and their integration emerges out of the earliest psychic process in the relation of the infant and the mother and continues to exist in addition to the familiar id-ego-superego structure of the psyche in Freudian and object relations theories of self. Kohut suggests that the child has two

---

ner. He argues that under favorable circumstances, narcissism may be transformed as creativity, empathy, acknowledgment of mortality, humor, and wisdom. See Kohut, "Forms and Transformations of Narcissism," in *Essential Papers on Narcissism,* ed. Andrew P. Morrison (New York: New York University Press, 1986), 61–87; and also Lynn Layton and Barbara Ann Schapiro, eds., *Narcissism and the Text: Studies in Literature and the Psychology of the Self* (New York: New York University Press, 1986), 2–27.

39. Kohut identifies environmental factors as not only gross events and broadly outlined factors from early life during childhood "but also—and principally—the pervasive influence of the personalities of the parents and of the atmosphere in which the child grew up, which, singly or in combination with each other, account for the specific characteristics of the nuclear self and for its firmness, weakness, or vulnerability." *Restoration of the Self, 187.*

opportunities to move toward consolidation of the self and notes that pathological self disturbance occurs only if both of these developmental opportunities fail. The first opportunity concerns the child's grandiosity mirrored in the empathically responding "merging-mirroring-approving self-object" to form a cohesive grandiose-exhibitionistic self. The second opportunity concerns the child's relation to the empathically responding parent who enjoys the child's merger and idealization, forming a cohesive idealized parent imago. Kohut suggests that if there is weakness in one constituent of the bipolar self, it may be compensated for by the development of strength in the other.[40]

Continuity of the self occurs despite changes in body, personality, and surroundings, as a firmly "cohesive nuclear self" enables us to maintain a sense of our enduring identity, according to Kohut. This continuity emanates not only from the "content of the constituents" in the two poles of the nuclear self and the "activities" resulting from the tensions in the bipolar self but also from the relation in which the constituents stand to each other. Kohut identifies this relationship between the poles (ambitions and ideals) as a "tension gradient" that is specific for the individual "even in the absence of any specific activity between the two poles of the self."[41] Kohut contends that this tension gradient exists as an "action-promoting condition" distinguished from the "tension arc" or abiding flow of actual psychological activity between the two poles as a person is "driven" by ambitions and "led" by ideals. In this way, Kohut's theory identifies more specifically the continuity in the structure of the nuclear self, a relation or tension gradient that Kohut identifies as "conditions."

A sense of continuity and enduring identity may have more to do with the individual, unchanging specificity of the relation between the two poles, which has abiding significance, in this theory of self:

> ...our sense of abiding sameness within a framework of reality that imposes on us the limits of time, change, and ultimate transience is not based entirely on the lifelong sameness of our basic ambitions and ideals—even these will sometimes change without an ensuing loss of our sense of continuity. It may ultimately be, not the content of the nuclear self, but the unchanging specificity of the self-expressive, creative tensions that point toward the future—which tells us that our transient individuality also possesses a significance that extends beyond the borders of our life.[42]

---

40. Ibid., 185.
41. Ibid., 180.
42. Ibid., 182.

The self's sense of continuity through time results from the abiding action-promoting tension gradient between the two major constituents of the nuclear self, which is "laid down" in early childhood. On the basis of this hypothesis, Kohut suggests that the restoration of a fragmented self (narcissistic disturbance in the nuclear self) is complete when the individual disengages from the "working-through processes of ill-functioning structure."[43] Kohut further distinguishes this process of restoration by suggesting that recovery of childhood memories comes to an end when "the sense of abiding sameness of the self along the time axis" has been established,[44] that is, when remembering has served its purpose of strengthening the coherence of the self. A primary task of analysis is sufficient reconstruction of pathogenic features of parents and early childhood atmosphere to establish a "dynamic connection" with current distortions in personality.

One of the radical shifts that distinguishes Kohut's perspective from object relations theory is his insistence upon the relation between the self and its self-objects as the essence of psychological life.[45] Rather than relinquishing self-objects for love objects or moving from narcissism to object love, he argues that psychological health involves the achievement of self-cohesion and that therapy involves healing of a formerly fragmented self. He maintains that psychologically healthy adults continue to need mirroring of the self by self-objects and persons appropriate for idealization. Kohut defines mental health "not only as freedom from the neurotic symptoms and inhibitions that interfere with the functions of a mental apparatus involved in loving and working, but also as the capacity of a firm self to avail itself of the talents and skills at an individual's disposal, enabling him to love and work successfully."[46]

The implications of this brief summary for an adequate theory of self informed by feminist theory in pastoral care and counseling can be focused on two particular issues. The first issue concerns psychology as a means for understanding human experience and the specific form or structure of the inner self as it is laid down in early childhood. What parts of the nuclear self have consistency over time and in spite of changes in other aspects of the self or the environment? As distinguished from social-construction theory of self, understanding the consistency or continuity

---

43. Ibid., 183.
44. Ibid.
45. Kohut, *How Does Analysis Cure?* 47.
46. Kohut, *Restoration of the Self,* 284.

of the self does not make change less possible but suggests some limit to social influence and the possibility of creative self-expression. Provided that one does not swing the pendulum back toward inattention to social and cultural forces, this perspective offers some affirmation of individual freedom.

The unique contribution of this theory to the tasks of pastoral care and counseling influenced by feminist theory is that self-expressive, creative tensions in the self-structure are characterized by unchanging specificity and point toward the future. Kohut develops this thought in terms of the transformation of narcissism in creativity, empathy, recognition of mortality, humor, and wisdom. For a psychologically healthy person, an internal condition that is enduring and specific to that individual is transformed through self-expression, transcending individuality and going beyond the transient border of the person's life. Social influences in the formation of the self during infancy through which the core self is "laid down" provide a basis for the specificity and particularity in the individual's self-expression.

A second issue concerns psychotherapy as a process of change, alleviating pathological distortion but also informing preventive care and maintaining mental health. Empathy and mirroring are tools for both psychotherapy and preventive care. As a means to facilitate healing of a "structural" deficiency in the self and a tool for restoration of the self, *empathy* means demonstrating regard for another's subjectivity, validating another's own understanding of his or her inner reality, and being willing to function as self-object in order to enhance another's development. A healthy self is free to act on its own initiative, with an expression of self that is unique to that individual, and Kohut's theory offers support for pastoral care and counseling seeking to affirm and enhance a person's freedom. Understanding another person on the basis of his or her internal experience, what Kohut calls "empathy," involves a specific perspective on that experience, a kind of "vicarious introspection" that nonetheless maintains the stance of an "objective observer."[47] Kohut claims, not that his self psychology introduces a new kind of empathy, but that it supplies a theory that broadens and deepens the field of empathic perception. I argue that empathy—the capacity to resonate with the inner life of an-

---

47. Kohut, *How Does Analysis Cure?* 175. The self-object transferences that occur during the analytic process, and which are empathically understood by the analyst, are "a new edition of the relation between the self and its self-objects in early life." Ibid., 173.

other while maintaining a particular perspective—is more possible when the interdependent self is sufficiently coherent and differentiated.[48]

Kohut stresses the importance of the conceptual separation between experience-distant abstractions and experience-near acts—grasping and responding to the other person's experience as that individual experiences it, separate from the analyst's conceptualization of what is "normal" or "in accord with" the person's structural "design":

> All meaningful human interactions, specifically those between parent qua selfobject [sic] and child and between analyst qua selfobject and analysand, are not only broad in the sense of applying to a variety of experiences, but deep in the sense of being in contact with early, and, in form, archaic, experiences. When a friend puts his arm around our shoulder at the moment we need to be sustained by him, he does not know that his gesture implies a willingness to let us merge with the calmness and strength of his body, just as the selfobject mother once provided us with this experience when she lifted us, anxious and fragmenting, and held us to her. And the same thing happens between analyst and analysand. However objective and limit-recognizing an analyst's interpretations may be, if they are preceded by understanding and deepen the analysand's recognition that he has been understood, then the old reassurance of a merger-bond, even on archaic levels, will reverberate, if ever so faintly, with the experience.[49]

Many feminist theological perspectives emphasize communal relations and understand the self to be foundationally social. The theory of self I am commending allows an individualist to be in community and to experience connection and interdependence without loss of self or experiencing alteration in the "core" self through social interaction or environmental change. The question is not only the individual's social interdependence and connections with other persons and social structures. A more complete theory of self recognizes the interdependent

---

48. Kohut discusses the "objective observer" in terms of a perspective on the particular aspect of reality with which one works in psychoanalysis, quite distinct from a kind of cold or distant stance. Using a metaphor of artistic perspective in painting, Kohut suggests that self psychology permits a perception of formerly unrecognized configurations that increase awareness of the significance of these configurations. Rather than disapproving of these, or in any way suggesting that the person is confusing the present and the past or mixing the therapist up with his or her parents, Kohut maintains that empathy is communicated as understanding of the other's inner experience. Empathy enables the other to recognize the significance of internal self-objects precisely because the analyst has not interfered with use of himself or herself as self-object. See *How Does Analysis Cure?* 175–76.

49. Ibid., 190–91.

structure of relations, the necessity for sufficient differentiation of self in these relations, and a notion of the inner self, at least a core part of which is not changed through social or contextual influence or interaction. Such a perspective enhances individual freedom and agency and affirms capacity for choice and expression of the individual self. Further, feminist theology or psychology that theorizes in terms of individual and communal, without a sense of continuity in the inner core of the self, may either underestimate the individual's freedom and agency or overestimate the power of social structure and process, or both.

Paradoxes in Feminist Theory

Within feminist theories are apparent contradictions regarding the use of a rhetoric of oppression because it may overgeneralize about women's experience and miss the particularity of race, economic class, and other specific aspects of human experience. The additional hazard of a rhetoric of oppression is that it may render an individual less able to claim agency, the capacity to act and influence a situation, changing it for the better. At issue is the tensive relationship between a particular individual, with a coherent identity, and the collective identity as "oppressed," which only partially identifies the person.

An emphasis on difference, on the other hand, may serve to revalue bodily experience, sensuality, and nurture based on women's experience.[50] The hazard of this strategy is that physical experience becomes overdeterminative; that is, the ambiguity and diversity of bodily experiences are overlooked in an idealized portrayal, and freedom is thus diminished. An emphasis on difference may be exaggerated into "alpha bias," as it has been called by some theorists who contend that such bias

---

50. Hawkesworth notes that the word "difference" is used in at least two distinct ways in feminist analysis. One usage is to identify supposed differences between men and women in order to value positively those that are uniquely female. This is the primary way Hawkesworth uses the term in her typology of rhetorical strategies. The second usage of the word is by feminist scholars in the postmodern tradition as they are informed by the theory of deconstruction. In postmodern thought, the "play of differences" within each gendered subject is used as a subversive strategy and refusal of difference as binary opposition between genders. Hawkesworth suggests that this second usage of "difference," conscious of the ideological power of language, is closer to the fourth rhetorical strategy, the rhetoric of vision. Marilyn E. Hawkesworth, *Beyond Oppression: Feminist Theory and Political Strategy* (New York: Continuum, 1990), 226.

contributes to political conservatism in the psychology of women.[51] Alpha bias views women and men as basically different and emphasizes this difference, whereas beta bias construes women and men as basically the same, attending to what they have in common. Alpha bias is thought to focus psychologists' attention on the individual personalities of women and men, and away from the social structures and context that help to shape personality. Beta bias, on the other hand, assumes that women and men are basically similar and that apparent gender differences are due to social forces that have a different affect on women and men. The result of alpha bias is that insufficient attention is given to external factors, such as the historical, political, and cultural forces that reinforce gender patterns:

> . . . a psychology of women that assumes that women and men are naturally different (alpha bias) or that differences are caused by factors internal to individuals (i.e., biological or socialized) is necessarily supportive of the status quo and, hence, antithetical to a women's movement. In contrast, we believe that a psychology that assumes apparent gender differences are the result of differential social forces supports a women's movement by identifying targets for social change.[52]

One theorist argues that psychology helps maintain the status quo of society when it endorses and reflects dominant social values and disseminates these values in the form of supposed "value-free" science. This conservative effect is particularly apparent in the psychology of women when gender difference is portrayed as person-based and immutable.[53] Described as "individualistic approaches," theories proposed by Carol Gilligan and Mary Belenky, among others, are noted for attributing gender difference to inherent, biological, or early socialization,

---

51. Rachel T. Hare-Mustin and Jeanne Marecek, "The Meaning of Difference: Gender Theory, Postmodernism, and Psychology," *American Psychologist* 43 (1988): 455–64, as cited in Arnold S. Kahn and Janice D. Yoder, "The Psychology of Women and Conservatism: Rediscovering Social Change," *Psychology of Women Quarterly* 13 (1989). Kahn and Yoder cite the work of Gilligan and that of Mary F. Belenky, among others, as illustrative of alpha bias. Chodorow's work on mothering is noted as an example of alpha bias, but with the exception that she recognizes external factors influencing behavior and theorizes that capitalism, not socialization, is a primary cause of gender-stereotyped development. Thus, according to Kahn and Yoder, the conservative political outcome of alpha bias is avoided in Chodorow's thought, as in Nancy Chodorow, *The Reproduction of Mothering: Psychoanalysis and the Sociology of Gender* (Berkeley: University of California Press, 1978).

52. Kahn and Yoder, "The Psychology of Women and Conservatism," 428.

53. Ibid., 424–25. The authors cite the work of I. Prilleltensky, "Psychology and the Status Quo," *American Psychologist* 44 (1989): 800.

thus rendering these differences resistant to change. It may be more accurate to say that psychological theory is inadequate if it is based only on gender difference. An alternative understanding suggests that freedom is enhanced by attention to individual differences among men and among women, as well as to the commonalities among men and women, or any categories of human experience in addition to gender. From this perspective it is important to identify the consistency and stability of the self that is not subject to social relationship or determined solely by cultural influence, as I have suggested in drawing from Kohut's self psychology.

To understand self in broader terms than its vulnerability to social influence is particularly desirable in a patriarchal culture. Theorizing about the consistency of stability of the inner self and possibilities for self-initiated action serves to limit an overdetermining sense of embeddedness in interstructured relations. Whereas innate drives and biological capacities were considered determinative in the past, I argue that analysis of social and cultural influences has now extended into a kind of overdetermining power and that a rebalancing of perspectives on the self is needed. In this manner, theorizing from diversity does not preclude attention to the continuity of the individual self and is in fact enhanced through understanding the particularity of individual experience as it both reflects and contradicts generalizations based on categories of gender, race, and the like.

Historian Elizabeth Fox-Genovese discusses contradictions within feminism as claims for absolute equality are made along with claims for protection based on distinctly female experience.[54] She views this as an inconsistency in means toward valid ends and frames her argument in terms of the inadequacy of individualist theory as a basis for decision making. She also sees a danger in radical individualism, which makes collective identity or action impossible and instead commends individual freedom grounded in the discipline of the collectivity, or community. However, Fox-Genovese does not state how the collectivity or community will take into account competing claims in order to arrive at a vision of the common good. If the collectivity or community is understood to be religious or state structures and institutions, how will they more effectively overcome past discrimination or manage resources with more justice? While her argument does not resolve this dilemma, it is nonetheless pertinent to this project as a reminder of the diversity of views within feminism regard-

---

54. Elizabeth Fox-Genovese, *Feminism without Illusions: A Critique of Individualism* (Chapel Hill: University of North Carolina Press, 1991).

ing the most desirable relation of individual and communal or collective values and purposes.

From a pastoral theological perspective, Fox-Genovese's argument points to the tension between benefiting from participation in the church and its tradition and at the same time criticizing church and tradition on the basis of experience so that harm will not be perpetuated. From my point of view, the church as a religious institution is and must continue to struggle with affirmative action for women and minorities and must develop intentional, mandatory efforts to educate leadership in responsible, ethical behavior and healthy interpersonal boundaries. Illustrated in this way, claims to equality and to "protection" in the form of preventing harm are not contradictory.

Practice of ministry is value laden and, as it portrayed in this project, intent upon framing experience toward the possibility of fuller responsiveness to God's presence and activity. I have claimed that many careseekers bring a faith perspective to a process of pastoral care and am promoting a collaborative relationship in which the careseeker's perspective is privileged as a problematic situation is understood and desired change identified. It may be accurate to say that pastoral care maintains the status quo of society and reflects dominant social and religious values. And yet I believe that feminist theological and therapeutic revisions in pastoral care and counseling conserve or maintain faith when it is difficult to do so, as well as change or transform individuals, groups, and society itself in response to God. Further, pastoral ministry influenced by feminist thought is more likely to use power on behalf of justice and compassion.

Construing oppression as an opportunity for appropriate resistance as a practice of faith may encourage people to do what they are able in changing themselves and their situations. This emphasis on agency serves to qualify the definition of self in terms of the limiting conditions of oppression, while affirming the possibility of joint efforts and communal strategies for addressing the causes of oppression. The Ballou and Gabalac model of separation from harm and health maintenance supports this notion of agency and accurately portrays the expressions of and working through anger and conflict that may be a part of resistance as a faithful response to oppression.

The theme of connection offers an interpretive tool for holding together what were thought to be contradictory strivings for remaining in relationship and being a distinct self. Connection may be discussed in terms of association, and of finding acceptance in community with others in order to work for change, provided that such association includes diverse values and experiences, with tolerance for difference. I have drawn from Gilligan's theory to clarify limits and possibilities in understanding the self's formation through social relationship. Understanding the "link" of interdependence between the self and a group or context helps caregivers to encourage desirable change to the extent that an individual critically perceives sociocultural context as more relative, contingent, and itself subject to change. In this way, greater critical awareness of the context in which the self is formed and continues to be influenced offers a more accurate assessment of problems encountered and the influence that may be brought to bear in response.

In these first three chapters I have engaged the task of pastoral theology as critical and constructive reflection on sources of knowledge that shape a ministry of pastoral care and counseling and offered a rationale for the sources selected based on a praxis method. I have discussed my social location as caregiver and theologian, the faith commitments that prompt this exploration, a religious tradition as interpreted by several theologians with attention to the themes identified, and the supporting disciplines of psychology and psychotherapy as interpreted by several theorists. Numerous references have been made to practice of ministry as the beginning point for the questions addressed in this effort. Pastoral theology has an empirical base and employs pragmatic criteria that assume action is important for theology. Unlike theology apart from praxis, which may involve study and inquiry at a theoretical level alone, examining and comparing concepts, pastoral theology attends to concrete situations and involves criteria for change and effectiveness in lived experience. In chapter 4, I focus more specifically on this fifth source of knowledge in the work of pastoral theology, that is, the practice of ministry through care, counseling, and consultation.

Chapter Four

Illustrations from the Practice of Ministry

A more adequate response to suffering and participation in its alleviation is possible when feminist theory informs ministries of care. Exploring this hypothesis, I have suggested that relational themes of response to God, resistance to harm, and interdependent connection help to make sense of the particular suffering that occurs in the structures of power in contemporary culture.

Identifying problems as they emerge in ministry and analyzing them from various theological perspectives involves a systematic process of reflection, often employing psychological and political theory from supporting disciplines. Pastoral theology claims that a therapeutic process occurs in the wider presence of God and that God may participate in healing and change through a variety of means, including pastoral care. Pastoral counseling often includes an assessment of spiritual history, sense of relation to God, and current practice of faith as part of an initial definition of a problem and identification of strengths and resources for addressing it. At the same time, a pastoral counselor perceives present problems and diagnostic categories in the larger framework of spiritual, family, social, and cultural factors influencing the person, drawing from critical theory to aid in this wider scope.

A research design based on the scientific method cannot account for all the variables a pastoral counselor assumes are at work in the process of change, and this limitation implies that what pastoral caregivers and counselors do is more art than science. But both art and science involve skills that can be learned. To the extent that caregiving, counseling, and consultation can be observed and analyzed, and a systematic understanding or knowledge gleaned from this observation, a practice of ministry can be thought of as "science," something which can be known. Practice of ministry is understood here as a combination of art and science, integrating creative skill and empirical study so that reasoned evaluation of and improvement in practice can occur.

In this chapter I focus on material from my practice of care, counseling, and consultation in order to illustrate and explore the hypothesis of this project. Before summarizing this material, I want to comment on the significance of a case study approach.[1] The difficulties in defining concepts and terms for empirical study in pastoral care involve feelings and relationships that may not be rendered observable or measurable in ways that are immediately conducive to experimental research. Choosing a case study approach implies regard for the credibility of subjective experience and self-report of change in behavior or circumstance. Attempting a "quasi-experimental" research design would mean hypothesizing a significant difference in outcome of care influenced by feminist theory and establishing some controls for this practice of ministry as an independent variable and for the outcome of a caring process (based on caregiver and careseeker reports from interview and questionnaire) as a dependent variable. As an alternative, I define the scope of empirical research for this project in terms of "clinical significance," with no intention of establishing statistical significance. This approach, based on case study material, allows continuing definition of key elements in pastoral care informed by feminist theory, with an open-ended outcome that invites further study. In this way, my intention is to affirm empirical study of several aspects of pastoral ministry and to participate in critical and constructive evaluation of a specific type of pastoral care.

In presenting illustrative case material, I draw from pastoral relationships in my current practice of pastoral counseling in the context of a divinity school pastoral care center, as well as previous pastoral experiences in congregations.[2] In the first three parts of this chapter, I present case studies of individual, family, and congregational situations of need

---

1. Current conversation regarding qualitative and quantitative methods of empirical research in pastoral counseling is explored in James McHolland, ed., *The Future of Pastoral Counseling: Whom, How, and For What Do We Train* (Fairfax, Va.: American Association of Pastoral Counselors, 1993). For many years I relied on the diagnostic categories identified in Paul Pruyser's, *The Minister as Diagnostician* (Philadelphia: Westminster Press, 1976). These categories are awareness of the holy, providence, faith, grace or gratefulness, repentance, communion, and sense of vocation. More recently I have explored the multidimensional, functional approach commended in George Fitchett, *Assessing Spiritual Needs: A Guide for Caregivers* (Minneapolis: Augsburg, 1993). This 7 x 7 model explores person and context in seven holistic dimensions and seven dimensions of spirituality in order to develop an informed pastoral care plan.

2. As noted earlier, names and other identifying information have been changed, and composite portrayals of a variety of individuals, groups, and congregations are used in order to maintain the confidentiality of pastoral relationships.

and brief verbatim material in order to demonstrate the process of care and the influence of feminist revisions. The final section of the chapter affirms that care, counseling, and consultation are informed, but not overtaken, by the paradigms of therapeutic, political, and social theories and are primarily theological endeavors that seek to reflect and anticipate God's activity. I argue that in selected situations pastoral ministry informed by feminist theological and therapeutic sources offers a more accurate and effective pastoral response to need than pastoral ministry not informed by feminist sources.

Pastoral Care in Response to Crisis

One of the vignettes with which this book began portrayed a pastoral encounter with Clive, a fifty-year-old man hospitalized for heart bypass surgery. Clive was a key leader in the congregation, known for his skill as an investor and for his good sense of humor. He had worked closely with the pastor on several stewardship efforts, functioning as an effective spokesperson on behalf of benevolence giving and the long-range plans of the congregation. Clive had sought conversation of a different sort with the pastor at the point when his first marriage was in crisis and accepted a referral for marriage counseling with a therapist whom the pastor recommended. Clive and Rhonda, his first wife, had worked hard to recover their covenant relationship, but following a year of separation, they came to a mutual agreement that divorce was the best option. Rhonda chose to join another congregation, and Clive remained active in the church in which he had grown up and where his mother still attended. A few months after the divorce, Clive and Gloria, who had known one another socially for several years, were married in a private ceremony led by the pastor. Clive's son and daughter, ages sixteen and eighteen, and Gloria's daughter, age fourteen, were included in the ceremony, and Gloria's daughter chose to live with Gloria and Clive.

Premarital counseling had included conversation about their respective first marriages and what they had learned about themselves through the difficult experience of divorce. Gloria spoke of learning that she was stronger than she had thought and what a shock it had been when her first husband filed for divorce. She had made a special effort to encourage her daughter to continue a solid relationship with her first husband, taking care to work through her own anger at him with friends rather than through her daughter. Gloria felt she had managed a devastating situation with some courage and resilience. She saw herself differently in partnership with Clive, with more "self-respect," and Clive joked a bit about how "tough" it was to live with a strong woman.

Clive had spoken openly of his decision to stop drinking in the pre-marital counseling process with the pastor. He did not think he was an alcoholic, but he knew that his problematic use and occasional abuse of alcohol had interfered with his relationship with Rhonda and his children. Clive expressed regret that he had not acknowledged this earlier, but he also maintained that his use of alcohol was more a symptom than a cause of the problems with Rhonda, one of several points on which they had disagreed. He said it was easier to talk with Gloria and a great relief to be in a relationship in which he didn't feel he needed to defend himself all the time. They both expressed gratitude for being able to make a fresh start and surprise at how good it felt to experience affection and companionship again.

Several weeks after Clive's surgery, he was at the church for a committee meeting and engaged the pastor on an issue that had met with opposition by a majority of the members. Clive then turned the conversation in a different direction:

CLIVE: You know, I've been wanting to talk with you about that sermon you preached a couple weeks ago, the one about the rich fool building more barns just before he dies.

PASTOR: Yeah, those Advent texts can be pretty fierce.

CLIVE: Well, that one got to me. I hadn't heard it that way before. [Pauses] I remember when you came to visit me in the hospital. I didn't tell you at the time, but I had this sense that I could be dead and you were there to give me last rites or something.

PASTOR: Wow, I didn't mean to scare you.

CLIVE: I know. Believe me, I'm glad I'm still here walking around, but I haven't been the same since. And then that sermon about the fool who had his priorities screwed up. You know, I was only twenty-four years old when my Dad died.

PASTOR: Yes, I remember your mother telling me once that it was very sudden.

CLIVE: (Tearful) I was pretty broken up about it, but I tried to be there for my mom. But it's like I'm stuck now with this sense of dying just at the point when things are going so well.

PASTOR: So even though your doctor says you're doing great, there's this sense that you could die suddenly, like your father did.

CLIVE: Right. And it's like I've been a fool, or fooling myself. I don't know, it feels strange to be talking this way. Something has changed. I've talked with Gloria about it some, tried to, anyway. I don't want to make the same mistakes and pretend I can manage everything on my own. She's been great about listening to me, and it scared her when I wound up in the hospital.

PASTOR: I'm thankful you two have one another. But something has changed for you.

CLIVE: It's like I don't know myself, or I don't recognize myself. I can't even tell a good joke when I need to right now. And I'd love to buy a bottle of scotch and just bury it, just try to forget about it. But I'm not going to do that. I can't go back to the way things were before.

PASTOR: You're looking for a different way to manage a tough time.

CLIVE: Yes, I want to stick with what's new in my life, and I know if I head down that path again I'd just be making things the way they were. I'm stronger than that, at least I think I am.

PASTOR: How *did* you manage to make a fresh start? You and Gloria talked about that before your wedding, that there was something different happening for both of you, and part of it was sharing the load.

CLIVE: That's true. We have a different kind of marriage than either of us had before, and it's been great. I guess I've trusted her with more, the things I worry about, stuff that wakes me up in the middle of the night.

PASTOR: Then part of what's changed is that you're not keeping so much to yourself.

CLIVE: Right, but it's more than that. It's like a relief to not be responsible for everything, to not have to take the lead with everything. Even at work I notice a difference. Between what my Dad left us and the stock market, we're well set, and I'm not as worried about the future as I used to be.

PASTOR: So your marriage is secure, your financial situation is secure, but something else is unsettling you right now.

CLIVE: Why did I hear myself in that story of the rich fool? I felt stupid, thinking I could be dead and none of it mattered.

PASTOR: None of it mattered?

CLIVE: That there's something else I need to do before I die. (Pauses) This is ridiculous. You know how much I've done.

PASTOR: Yes, I know you've achieved a lot. But it sounds like something's going on, something's shifting for you, and that you're paying attention to it. I can't help wondering what the wise version would be. I mean you've talked about feeling stupid, identifying with the fool, as if God is judging you, and I'm thinking, "Where's the wisdom here, the part about storing treasures in the right place?"

CLIVE: That was the point, wasn't it? I'm a smart guy; I should know this.

PASTOR: Well yes, but you've been through a crisis. I mean people change when they go through something life-threatening, like you have. Especially remembering how your father died, what you've gone through can call a lot into question. That makes sense to me.

CLIVE: But the health crisis is past, so what's the problem?

PASTOR: I'm not sure I can name it for you, but I keep thinking this is important, it's not something to be buried, and that you're on the right track talking with Gloria about it, forgoing the scotch. And hearing the parable in a different way and telling me about it . . . there's some wisdom in what you're doing right now. And it's different from what you would have done in the past.

CLIVE: So you don't think the rich fool image fits? (They laugh)

PASTOR: Well, no, I hadn't thought of you that way, but that story obviously struck something in you, and in a way, I'm thankful to hear you wrestling with it, hard as it sounds. I mean, my hunch is that's the way God works, sort of sneaking up on us sometimes, catching us by surprise, and it's unnerving how we're changed by it.

CLIVE: Changed for the better?

PASTOR: We hope.

CLIVE: So you think God's up to something here, working on me?

PASTOR: That's what it sounds like to me—some wisdom to be gleaned in all this.

CLIVE: Yeah, well, just make sure you don't preach any more sermons like that for a while. I can't take it.

PASTOR: Okay. Okay.

The pastor and Clive talked a while longer and agreed to meet again in a couple weeks to see what further thoughts Clive had about his situation. She encouraged Clive to think about a "wise" version of a man who is secure in many ways and yet understandably unsettled by a crisis. The pastor felt privileged that Clive had chosen to speak with her about the effect of the hospital visit and trusted her with some of his feelings, quite different from the usual encounters with Clive in which he offered *her* support and always made a humorous comment or two.

Numerous interpretations of this pastoral encounter could be made, and the following analysis leaves a great deal unsaid in a selective focus on the themes of this project. Pastoral theological reflection on this situation of care begins with the context of a congregation in which Clive was consistently perceived as a powerful person and well respected for the choices he made in using that influence on behalf of the good of the church and the local community. The continuity of the pastoral relationship over several years and the context of a caring community make a difference in the pastoral response to Clive's crisis. The response of care was surely not limited to what the pastor offered, and there were many witnesses to both brokenness and sacredness in that community of faith. Many in the congregation had grieved the end of Clive and Rhonda's marriage, took care to engage and nurture their children through a difficult time, and felt joy when it appeared that Clive and Rhonda were moving on to new relationships and their respective new commitments of marriage. Likewise, many members of the congregation extended care to Clive and his family at the time of his surgery and recovery, and those of his parent's generation recollected the shock of his father's death years ago.

In a way, Clive's vulnerability was exposed through the process of divorce and in his more recent health crisis, both quite "public" events for the congregation. For Clive, a person accustomed to power in the sense of the ability and authority to act and to influence, the failure of his first marriage and the blockage in his heart were challenges that clarified exercise of power through interdependence. Initially, Clive seemed to associate vulnerability with powerlessness, feeling like a fool or uncharacteristically "stupid." Nonetheless, he benefited from the congregation's responses of care and found a way to trust Gloria and a few others with some of his internal process of grieving multiple losses. These connections, more interdependent than he had recognized them to be, proved vital to his altered sense of "place," a part of the wisdom that he came to articulate.

The language of "demand" in Luke's parable of the rich fool (12:13–21 NRSV) was part of what so unsettled Clive in hearing the Advent sermon. The parable portrayed God's power in the harsh language of "demanding" the fool's life because the man had been greedy and stored up possessions rather than being "rich toward God." Clive came to understand that this fit well with his memory of his father's life being abruptly "taken away," and resolving anger toward God about this loss was a task of grieving that Clive did not welcome but tried to work through. In the process, it became clearer that Clive was not "doing" something wrong or being greedy as much as needing to "be" in a different "place" in the larger scheme of things. Clive had managed to use power without dominating others either in his family or in his work, a pattern he had learned from his own father. He had taken on a great deal of responsibility in both spheres and skillfully functioned as a leader who was able to delegate to and work with others in a respectful manner. Interdependence and a sense of "partnership" with Gloria were new ways of thinking about significant relationships, and Clive expressed some relief and gratitude for not having to shoulder so much responsibility alone.

At the same time, portrayal of God's power as domination—judging, demanding, unmerciful—was disturbing to Clive as he heard the story of God's response to the rich fool in a new way. He thought it was very unfair that the rich fool didn't get a second chance or hadn't understood quite how things were and so was ignorant of the gravity of his situation. Other Scripture portrays God as gracious and merciful in ways that were much more appealing, and yet part of the point of the text in question seems to be God's freedom in relation to humanity, God's insistence upon relationship with us, even God's anger that the fool's desires had turned elsewhere. Viewed in this light, as God's response to refusal of relationship, the text still seemed harsh to Clive but made more sense. Some of what changed for Clive was an altered sense of the contingency of life, the fragility of what we've made of ourselves, and a stronger sense of his own limits, mortality, and temporary "place" in the world. At the same time, he expressed gratitude for having a second chance, both in marriage and through his health crisis, to try again.

Clive's crisis resonates with some of Kohut's framework as it portrays healthy narcissism and its transformation as creativity, empathy, acknowledgment of mortality, humor, and wisdom. To the extent that an idealized parental imago functioned as a psychic construct for Clive, some of the disruption in his relation to God could be viewed as a disturbance in the association of this imago with God, whose power has been called into question by Clive's losses. The "action-promoting condition" between the two poles of the self as it is driven by ambitions and led by ideals was fragmented for a time as the mirroring function of the idealized parental imago, associated with his father and with God, was altered by the integration of a fuller sense of mortality and the transience of life. One could also conjecture that Clive was venturing into greater psychological health through a fuller transformation of healthy narcissism as he became more empathic in his most intimate relationships and sought a "wiser" version of how to live his life in the face of mortality and mystery. In this way, both continuity and change may have occurred in Clive's psychic structure and in his sense of himself, and his capacity for flexibility in interpersonal relations and in response to God was enhanced.

Perhaps the pastoral response to Clive could have occurred in exactly the same manner without any influence from feminist theory. However, I maintain that this influence strengthens a response to several issues in this pastoral encounter. The understanding of care as a ministry shared by all members of a congregation is a shift away from "clericalism" toward an affirmation of the formal and informal structures of care that have always existed in Christian community. I understand this to be one manifestation of God's presence and activity in a community of faith and one way in which a pastor is not "heroically" alone in offering care. Caregivers who view their role as part of a network of caring community are, I believe, less burdened with the need to get it all "right" and are less likely to overtake a careseeker's agency and capacity to act with their own need to be helpful. The mutuality of care, as it is now described in my own denomination, acknowledges and affirms the support that members of a congregation offer one another on a regular basis and especially in times of need or crisis.[3] Later in this chapter, I will discuss further implications of the themes of this project in relation to this illustration of pastoral care in response to crisis.

Pastoral Counseling and Agency

This project began with a glimpse of the situation Ray and Janet were facing as they described it to the pastor during a home visit. In this section, I will more fully present and evaluate the pastoral response to Ray and Janet, particularly as it occurred following their referral to a pastoral counselor. The pastor chose to refer Ray and Janet following a subsequent encounter with Janet in which she described Ray's increasing frustration with his employer, and with Janet herself and the children, and an acknowledgment that she was probably making things worse.

Prior to making the referral, the pastor called the counselor to assure that an appointment time would be available for them, confirmed that the sliding fee scale was still in effect, and related some information about the couple. He also indicated that he was referring them primarily due to his own time constraints, not because of the severity of their problems. Janet had been a member of the congregation for two years and attended occasionally, and the pastor indicated he did not know the couple well, although he had visited twice in their home, his only encounters with Ray. Ray was very polite when the pastor had visited but was not interested in participating in the church. He had immigrated from Mexico fifteen years before and had met and married Janet shortly after his arrival in

3. My denomination defines *nurture* and *pastoral care* as "mutual ministries of the church" that emerge from and are nourished by "the Word proclaimed and heard, by the Sacraments celebrated and received, and by prayer offered and shared in worship." Presbyterian Church (U.S.A.), "Directory for Worship," in *The Constitution of the Presbyterian Church (U.S.A.)*, part 2, *Book of Order* (Louisville: Office of the General Assembly, Presbyterian Church (U.S.A.), 1998–99), W-6.1000.

the United States. Janet was not close to her family of origin, and Ray's relatives who lived in the area had welcomed her into the extended family. Their two children seemed to enjoy being a part of "the cousins," as they called the group who "hung out" just a little apart from the grownups at frequent family gatherings. Janet had hoped that her two children would go through confirmation class, but they had resisted her efforts to involve them in church.

At the initial meeting with the pastoral counselor, Janet voiced her concern about Ray and how tired he was all the time. Janet said that Ray had always been very good to her and the children, a good husband and father, but that they were arguing more and having a lot less fun than they used to. She described how they used to go dancing all the time when they first met and that Ray even played guitar in a band for a while. She thought he was very romantic back then, and she said his family had treated her very well even though she "couldn't speak a word of Spanish." When asked what she hoped would be different as a result of counseling, Janet said she hoped Ray would be "more like his old self again" and not just watch TV at home. Asked what would change in their relationship if that occurred, she said maybe they could go out together like they used to or do something with the kids.

Ray, who had been silent as Janet spoke, said the only problem was that he worked very long hours at his construction job, and there was nothing he could do about it. He said it was getting harder to work twelve hours a day, six days a week, particularly in the heat of summer. His employer, "my Anglo boss," as Ray called him, had been sporadic in paying Ray and his coworkers but usually came through with a cash payment every few weeks. Because he did not have a high school education, Ray did not consider looking elsewhere for employment. Asked what he hoped would be different as a result of counseling, Ray said he didn't think they needed counseling, but he had agreed to come this once to see what it was like. The counselor affirmed his willingness to give it a try, even if it turned out to be this one time. Ray then volunteered that what he thought was going to be different was Janet if she went back to school, as she was talking about doing. The dialogue continued:

COUNSELOR: You think Janet is going to change if she goes back to school.

RAY: That's what I think. I know she wants things better than we have them, not just for herself, but for the kids.

JANET: I thought you wanted me to go back to school!

RAY: I want you to be happy. I don't think things are so bad right now.

JANET: But you said you thought it would be a good example for the kids if I did.

RAY: Yeah, that's true.

JANET: So what are you complaining about?

RAY: I'm not complaining. I just said what I thought would be different.

JANET: Yeah, me. You don't want me to go back to school because you think I'll be better than you if I do. (To counselor) I have a high school diploma, and he doesn't. Big deal. It doesn't make that much difference, Ray. You know I love you. I'm doing this to make things better for all of us.

COUNSELOR: (Pause) Let me see if I'm getting this. (To Janet) You're planning to go back to school, to...?

JANET: To community college.

COUNSELOR: ...so that you can get a better job.

JANET: Right. Where I'm working now, they just pay minimum wage. I can do better than that. The other place, it's real part time, just cash.

COUNSELOR: Okay. So you both agree that Janet going back to school is a good idea so you, Janet, have a better job and it helps the whole family. But I thought I heard some concern that that's not the only difference it would make? (Looking at Ray)

RAY: I think she'll change.

JANET: I won't change.

RAY: (Shakes his head)

JANET: School doesn't make that much difference.

RAY: It does to me.

JANET: Well, ... it does to me, too, but not the same way.

COUNSELOR: How does it make a difference for you, Janet?

JANET: He's afraid I'm going to change, that I won't respect him anymore. That's not true. I'm not going anywhere, Ray. You don't need to worry about me changing about you.

COUNSELOR: (To Ray) Do you want to respond?

RAY: (Pauses) I'm not against your going to school; I just hadn't expected it. We've always talked about the kids graduating and going to college. I'll do anything to make that happen. I just didn't expect you would.

JANET: Sometimes I still surprise you. I've prayed about this, you know. It's important to me. I think I can do this.

COUNSELOR: (To Janet) I'd like to hear more about your prayer about this. Let me just see if I heard what Ray said, and we'll come back to that. (To Ray) Did I understand that it's more a change in what you'd expected, sort of a shift in plans for your family? Is that what you mean?

RAY: Yeah, a shift between us.

COUNSELOR: Between you and Janet?

RAY: Right. It looks like she's the boss.

JANET: How can you say that? I don't boss you around. You know that. (To counselor) Do you see how we get into arguments all the time? Just turn on the damned TV, then. It doesn't do any good to argue.

COUNSELOR: Wait a minute. I want to make sure I'm following this. You were saying, Ray, that if Janet goes back to school, it would look like she's the boss between the two of you, like she's in charge in your family?

RAY: That's what I meant. I'm not saying she bosses me around. It's just hard for me. My brothers—they make jokes about this, about the wife running things.

COUNSELOR: So it's like you lose face in your family if it looks like Janet is running things, even if that's not really true between the two of you.

JANET: Well, that's true. Two of his brothers, they really are bad about that. I mean they're respectful and all, but they'll let you know if you overstep.

COUNSELOR: And Ray, you're saying your brothers would let you know if they thought you weren't in charge in your marriage or if you weren't sharing leadership with Janet?

RAY: Yeah.

JANET: I don't want to embarrass you in front of your family; I just want to go to school.

COUNSELOR: I guess I hadn't asked yet how you see power being shared between the two of you. Do you see one marriage partner having more than the other or about the same or what?

JANET: About the same.

RAY: Right.

COUNSELOR: Okay, well that's good to hear you both want the same thing, I mean, sharing the leadership of your family. I'm wondering how the two of you can work this out so that you (Janet) could go to school and you (Ray) can trust that neither one of you is "the" boss over the other. How do people know that about the two of you? (They offer views of how they work together as a "team" on parenting their children and providing for their family.)

COUNSELOR: So you do have a reference point, some good experience in sharing leadership in your family. I think the more details we can get about how you manage to do that, especially in two areas that are difficult for many couples—parenting and money—the more you'll be able to build on the strengths in your marriage. If I can go back to something you said earlier, Janet, it sounded important when you were saying that you've prayed about your situation. Are you open to saying a little more about that, what you've prayed for?

JANET: I started praying again when I joined the church. I wanted the kids to get a better start than I did, about being a Christian family and praying to Jesus. They didn't go for it, but I'm still trying.

COUNSELOR: There have been some disappointments with your children not getting involved, but you continue to pray to Jesus for...?

JANET: For the kids to be safe, to do the right thing, to not feel alone. I worry about them.

COUNSELOR: So you pray for protection for them, for Jesus to help them make good choices.

JANET: I've made a lot of mistakes in my life, and it's been better since I started saying a prayer in the morning, you know, to try to be a good mother and a good wife.

COUNSELOR: It helps to know that Jesus helps you with that.

JANET: It does help. He's by my side no matter what; that's the way I think about it now.

The first session continued with Ray and Janet specifying how they each know, and how others know, that they share "being the boss" in their family and strategizing how they could respond as a "team" if Ray's family members were critical of Janet's going back to school. At one point, Ray clarified that it wasn't only his brothers but also their children whose perceptions he was concerned about, not wanting to lose authority in their eyes if he and Janet were "more different" in level of education than they had been to this point. Ray and Janet were able to distinguish between level of education and capability for leadership in the family, so that the two qualities were not necessarily linked, and to imagine increased flexibility in leadership and participation by their children as the family tried to meet the new challenge of Janet's going to school. It was not *only* others' perceptions that Ray was concerned about, but improving their communication about power and authority in their relationship seemed to demonstrate to both of them that they were quite capable of enduring, and perhaps sometimes correcting, others' misperceptions.

Two weeks later, Ray and Janet returned for a second and final session in which they reported that Janet had registered for a class at the local community college, and Ray said they had not been arguing. Janet said she sort of missed making up afterwards, and the counselor wondered with them if it was possible to get the "afterwards" without the argument. They agreed to think about that. The possibility of returning for further counseling was left open, particularly as they met the challenge of Janet's being out two evenings a week and Ray's monitoring the children's activities while managing his own fatigue. One of the functions of the pastoral counselor in this situation was simply to slow the pace of interaction between Ray and Janet a bit around the particular issue they faced. Janet's quick responses to Ray and Ray's reticence in responding to Janet suggested that they ran into difficulty, in part, through their differences in pace. The counselor was aware that Ray might only engage in one session and chose to intervene in a way that sometimes interrupted their interaction for the sake of Janet's more accurately hearing what Ray had to say and inviting Ray to respond rather than remain silent.

Feminist theory strengthened the pastoral counseling response with this couple as flexible equity in the dynamics of power in their relationship was supported and encouraged. Agency, understood as power, influence, or the ability to act, became important in this pastoral counseling process because of the prospect of a power imbalance in the marital relationship and some echo of the misuse of power by Ray's boss. Resisting misuse of structured power could have been explicitly thematized with Ray and Janet if the counseling process had been extended, and suggesting appropriate resistance as one aspect of faithfulness to God might have resonated with their respective understandings of faith. Resisting misinterpretation of level of education as equivalent of power and authority within the family was also an affirmation of their view of shared leadership and interdependent relation. Notably, a regard for difference in interdependent relationship seemed to be demonstrated by Ray and his family in their acceptance of Janet even though her language and culture were "different," and they had accepted the burden of learning that different language in order to function in another culture. Several other implications of this illustration of pastoral counseling will be identified in the final section of this chapter.

Consultation for Caring Community

Pastoral care consultation is a relationship between (1) a caregiver and (2) a pastor, a group of pastors, a congregation, or several congregations in which the caregiver gathers information and offers advice regarding a particular situation of caregiving or building a program of care. I have included this form of pastoral care in this project because of the expressed need of pastors and congregations for this type of relationship with a person who is equipped to advise or guide others in caregiving and, in some instances, to collaborate in organizing and training persons for the care they will offer in their congregation. Bringing in an "outside" consultant is not always necessary, of course, but in my experiences as an interim pastor, and as a divinity school faculty member responding to pastors regarding the challenges they face, consultation as a form of pastoral care has taken on a significance that warrants attention. Case consultation and administrative or organizational consultation are two forms of this relationship, and the latter is the focus of this brief analysis.

Ample sources exist for exploring consultation with congregations based on family systems theory, and I do not replicate that material here.[4] I offer a brief and suggestive illustration of consultation in order more explicitly to add a feminist perspective to the mix of effective theory that already informs this aspect of pastoral care. Feminist theology and theory play a key role in shaping pastoral care consultation as a collaborative relationship and, through the themes explored in this project, offer several criteria that strengthen consultation as pastoral response to need. Further, I suggest that as pastoral care and counseling become less influenced by therapeutic theory that focuses exclusively on individuals and attends more fully to the structuring of power through social, cultural, and systemic influences upon individuals, families, and communal life, more accurate assessment of the multiple dimensions of problems will occur.[5] Pastoral consultation may foster a broader view of caring com-

---

4. Types of consultation are discussed in Gerald Caplan, *Theory and Practice of Mental Health Consultation* (New York: Basic Books, 1970). H. Newton Malony explores these types of consultation specific to pastoral counseling in "The Pastoral Counselor and Consultation Theory," *Journal of Pastoral Counseling* 12 (spring–summer 1977): 30–37. Other well-known resources in working with congregations as systems include Edwin H. Friedman, *Generation to Generation: Family Process in Church and Synagogue* (New York: Guilford Press, 1985); Pete Steinke, *Healthy Congregations: A Systems Approach* (Bethesda, Md.: Alban Institute, 1996); and *How Your Church Family Works: Understanding Congregations as Emotional Systems* (Washington, D.C.: Alban Institute, 1993); and Ronald W. Richardson, *Creating a Healthier Church: Family Systems Theory, Leadership, and Congregational Life* (Minneapolis: Fortress Press, 1996).

5. A similar point is well made by several pastoral theologians including Kathleen Billman, "Pastoral Care as an Art of Community," in *The Arts of Ministry: Feminist-Womanist Approaches,* ed. Christie Cozad Neuger (Louisville: Westminster

munity as highlighted in this illustration in order to lift up the "expertise" of lay leadership in discerning what caring means in a particular context at a specific time.

The First Community Church described in chapter 1 faced the discouraging prospect of declining membership, limited financial resources, and an uncertain future of pastoral leadership. The church was founded as a community of worship that valued its efforts in outreach ministry as an integral part of its identity. Through over four decades of its existence, the church had understood itself to be demonstrating the gospel as members identified patterns of need in the community and formed responses in a joint effort with two other churches in close proximity. The ecumenical relationships had been initiated through the relationship of the three pastors who met regularly as a small clergy association and who sought to be innovative and responsive in leading their congregations in the formation of a food and clothing bank for families in need, participation in building a home through Habitat for Humanity, and joint worship services once a month during the summer. As the membership of the First Community Church congregation began to decline over the past two decades from two hundred to the current roll of eighty, the pastors persisted in their ecumenical efforts to keep intact these significant outreach efforts, but with fewer and fewer members and declining availability of volunteers to maintain these projects, discouragement set in among the pastors and the congregations.

First Community's pastor did, in fact, accept a call to another congregation, and the board secured guest preachers for the Sunday worship service. After conversation with a representative from the denomination's area governing body, the board decided to use a consultant recommended to aid them in deciding how they could move forward until it was clear whether or not a new pastor would be called. Donna, the board member who had voiced a desire to move beyond a survival mentality, became chairperson of the board and facilitated the series of meetings with the consultant. She seemed to be the exception to this congregation's discouragement. As a thirty-year-old single woman, Donna was employed as a paralegal at a legal aid office in the metropolitan area close by and maintained her commitment to these efforts in an almost heroic effort to

John Knox, 1996), 10–38; Charles V. Gerkin, *Prophetic Pastoral Practice: A Christian Vision of Life Together* (Nashville: Abingdon, 1991), 116–42; and Larry Kent Graham, *Care of Persons, Care of Worlds: A Psychosystems Approach to Pastoral Care and Counseling* (Nashville: Abingdon, 1992).

lead her congregation in the absence of a pastor. She held out hope of attending law school so that she could better serve the clients who came to the legal aid office for assistance and was trying to save money for the right time to apply for admission.

After an initial process of becoming acquainted with the consultant, a problem-solving approach was implemented in which the board assessed the current concerns about maintenance of the facility, financial management, the part-time secretary and janitor positions, as well as the worship, Christian education, fellowship, and mission programs. The area of pastoral care emerged during a dialogue between two board members and the consultant about the congregation's mission outreach efforts in the following way:

DONNA: We had been visiting two families in the apartments across the street, especially when the grandmother became ill and they couldn't find a care center for her. I think she's still on a waiting list for a placement. I think that's outreach and caring both.

SAM: Those folks do need help, but I don't see how we can keep that up and still visit our own. I mean, it would be good if we could, but I don't see how we can do it all.

DONNA: But I don't think we should wait on these things till we have a new pastor. I think we should take seriously that we're all ministers; I mean we're not waiting for Moses to come down from the mountain. We can figure out where to go; can't we?

CONSULTANT: Funny you should mention that. I've heard this kind of transition time in a congregation compared to the Israelites' wilderness experience, in between where they'd been and didn't want to go back to and where they were going but hadn't arrived yet. The "in-between" times can be constructive, though, not just waiting.

SAM: No, we don't have to wait to do everything, but I still don't think we can manage what the pastor was doing by ourselves.

DONNA: Well, let's talk about what we *can* do. I mean, what *is* it possible for us to do? I'd rather take a more positive approach than wandering in the wilderness.

CONSULTANT: You were saying that helping the families across the street has been an important part of the mission and care of this church. Can you say a little more about why that's important here?

DONNA: I think it's part of who we are, part of our identity as a community church to be involved that way. It may not seem like much to someone from a large church who's used to doing more, but I think it's who we are, what we've been called to do here.

SAM: Our pastor had been working with the other two churches in town to try to do something together, like caring for a few of the kids who come home from school to an empty apartment, the churches taking turns helping with that. (Others add information and alternative views about this possibility.)

CONSULTANT: You have a broad perspective, among you, about this proposed ministry, the after-school program. It does sound like it continues the sense of identity you've had as a church that cares about your community, that gets involved in your community.

DONNA: That's why most of us are here, I think, because we wanted to be in that kind of church. I guess it's not for everybody, but I don't know how you can read about the early church and not do this. We just did a Bible study on that... One Body, One Spirit... about the gifts of the Spirit for building up the body of Christ.

CONSULTANT: Sounds helpful.

DONNA: I thought it was inspiring. I think it affirmed that we all have gifts and that we're called to use them.

CONSULTANT: So the Spirit is alive and well at First Community.

SAM: It's the adding-to-our-numbers part that hasn't worked so well.

CONSULTANT: Adding to our numbers?

SAM: That was supposed to be the result. You reach out, make an effort to invite people into the church, and they join so we don't keep going down. I mean, at the rate we're going, we're not even going to be here before long.

CONSULTANT: I see. You were hoping that the care you've been extending to the families across the street would lead to them joining the church.

SAM: That's what we thought would happen. But it's not going to help replace the windows or fix the bathroom that's closed now.

CONSULTANT: So the outreach efforts haven't solved the budget crunch or added to the membership roll.

DONNA: But that's not why we're doing it. I don't think we can look at it that way.

As the consultant continued to gather information from the board members and conducted a series of interviews with groups of other members of the church, it became clearer that there was a difference of opinion about whether to continue reaching out to persons in need in the community or to focus efforts on taking care of the membership of the church. It was not clear how much this difference of opinion reflected racism in the reluctance of some in this all-white congregation to encourage the African American families across the street to participate in their life as a church. Conversations with the other two churches in close proximity to First Community led to an ecumenical effort to begin an after-school program for neighborhood children, with the un-anticipated consequence of one extended family at First Community Church withdrawing their membership.

The inability to move forward and to demonstrate respect for the majority decision by the board was a disruption in the life of this community as it sought to broaden itself only to experience further diminishment in numbers. Nonetheless, this unfortunate event came to be understood as a time of faithfulness as this community of faith tried to reflect who God called them to be and to respond to what God called them to do. They began to speak much more of "caring community" than "sinking ship." As an illustration of one aspect of pastoral care that highlights the significant role of lay leadership in shaping and naming faithfulness, the exploration of their story will continue in the following section.

Beyond the Therapeutic Paradigm

An analysis of case material from practice of ministry will proceed as a kind of "thought experiment," to use Sallie McFague's term, discerning congruities and contradictions with the issues in theology previously explored. I will then assess the case material as it relates to the supporting discipline of psychology and therapeutic theory. My purpose in this analysis is to pause in the midst of praxis in pastoral care, counseling, and consultation so that theology more clearly determines or offers criteria for practice of ministry. I intend for theology to bring a specificity to practice, clarifying what forms of response to God, resistance, and connection are desirable and providing a more explicit theological context for these practices. In this way, pastoral care moves beyond the predominance of a therapeutic paradigm as a theory of change and is more fully character-ized as a theological endeavor.[6] At the same time, I will also identify points

---

6. In his discussion of the history of pastoral care and emerging new directions, Charles Gerkin identifies the need for more integration of the tasks of social trans-formation and commends a narrative hermeneutical model of pastoral care in which pastors function as interpretive guides. See Charles V. Gerkin, *An Introduction to Pastoral Care* (Nashville: Abingdon, 1997), 21–114. Gerkin draws from the typology of approaches in theology developed by George Lindbeck—propositional, experiential/expressive, and cultural-linguistic—and commends the latter approach as he develops his model. See George A. Lindbeck, *The Nature of Doctrine: Religion and Theology in a Postliberal Age* (Philadelphia: Westminster Press, 1984). In this project I have chosen a praxis method in order to identify the influence of feminist thought in pastoral care. One distinction between a narrative hermeneutical model for pastoral care and the

at which practice influences theory either as a correction in emphasis or as an unresolved issue in theory.

Three themes interpreted as anticipatory activity have emerged from my practice of ministry. I have identified these as faithful response to God, appropriate resistance to harm, and interdependent connections. Response to God becomes more faithful when it is based, not only on immediate need in subjective experience, but on a fuller representation of God as known through Scripture and a faith tradition or communal interpretation. Caregivers provide space for recollection and exploration of this fuller representation. We also encourage appropriate resistance and responsible action among careseekers through an understanding of the dynamics of power in the problematic situation and attempting congruence between the situation and the careseeker's agency. We affirm the careseekers' interdependence among a variety of connections with other persons, systems, and sociocultural influences as a theologically accurate understanding, provided that difference is regarded even as influence is claimed. When necessary, careseekers may achieve regard for difference through separation from harm, thereby diminishing the interdependent nature of a relation or connection. Healthy interdependent connections are characterized by empathy and compassion that respects difference on behalf of diversity and community, without reifying differences into opposition.

Caring for Relation to God

Clive was changed by the crisis he experienced and the convergence of grief over multiple losses, including his father's death years earlier, his first marriage, and a presumption of health. In a collaborative process of care, Clive articulated one element of grief in his response to a representation of God's power as dominance, an almost capricious misuse of power as Clive had heard it in the story of the rich fool. Initially, Clive associated this with his sense of his father's life being taken, abruptly, even capriciously, in the larger scheme of things, even as his own life could have been at the time of his surgery.

---

implications of a praxis method in pastoral theology is heightened attention to the consequences of practice, or what is "constructed" as a result. McFague makes a case for a theology that is not just hermeneutical but more fully constructive, or willing to think differently than in the past, with theological constructions as "houses to live in for a while, with windows partly open and doors ajar." Sallie McFague, *Models of God: Theology for an Ecological, Nuclear Age* (Philadelphia: Fortress Press, 1987), 21–28.

What brought about the change in Clive? From one perspective, the challenges to Clive's identity or subjective experience, his sense of being the same and managing coherence through the changes he had faced, finally tipped his balance, culminating in a revision of his relation and response to God. The caregiver validated Clive's sense of anger and vulnerability but chose not to reinforce Clive's interpretation of God's power as impulsive or erratic action. She attempted, instead, to hold together a notion of God's power as grace that does not cause individual illness or death as a kind of punishment but chooses to suffer with us when we face our creaturely limits. In this way, the caregiver tried to nurture a sufficient sense of continuity with Clive's faith as it had been shaped in a community and a tradition over many years and to invite some flexibility in Clive's response to God, with some revision of the faith he had inherited. From a theological perspective, the caregiver portrayed God's activity as freedom to draw close, as able to receive the anger and pain of grief, even to empathize with what feels to us like ultimate destructive power, and yet inviting the "odd" response of worship through the use of Psalms. Clive was not entirely satisfied with any explanation of the losses he had experienced, but finding a way to live well without having all the answers and to integrate more of the mystery of God's relation to the world into his faith was his task.

Clive experienced both continuity and disruption in his sense of himself through this crisis, continuing to confide in Gloria, active in the church and touching base with the pastor, resisting the pattern of alcohol abuse. One of the consequences of the crisis was Clive's attempt to change his interaction with his children, becoming more intentional in inviting conversation, rather than relying on affectionate teasing to communicate his love. His efforts did not meet with much "success," in his view, but some change in his sense of connection with them—a desire to be more open with them and to invite them to be more open with him—became important in a way it hadn't been before, despite his feeling awkward at first. From a developmental view, this desire could be characterized as generativity, as Clive tried to find a way to contribute to his children's lives in a way that fit more with their needs, even if it meant altering his preferred pattern of interaction in regard for his children's "different" preferences. The pastoral response to Clive illustrates care with an individual facing multiple challenges and portrays the ongoing significance of the function of care in nurturing individuals as they revise faithful response to God based on subjective experience interfacing with a faith tradition.

Counseling to Affirm Interdependence

The pastoral response to Ray and Janet in the form of a brief process of pastoral counseling suggests that analysis of the structuring of power in a marriage relationship and its wider social context requires "listening into" the dialogue for diverse dynamics of power. The fact that Ray and his family had welcomed Janet into their life was a very significant connection for her and provided a crucial experience of "belonging," which she did not experience in her original extended family. Further, the church Janet had joined had aided her rather nascent experience of faith and shaped her sense of identity and purpose in a personal relationship with Jesus, expressed through regular prayer, and the sense that Jesus was supporting and guiding her efforts to fulfill her roles as wife and mother. Both of these "systems," as well as the personal relationship with Jesus, provided influence that enhanced Janet's agency and her confidence in her ability to act on behalf of her own and her family's well-being. In this way, Janet was able to claim her power through healthy connections and sought to use it in a manner that benefited others as well as herself. Ray's brief references to his employer and to his brothers' different views regarding the role of a wife suggested that he was managing to resist the influence of power as dominance based on gender and race. Although Ray did not discuss problems of race or ethnicity as such, he appeared to be enduring a work situation in which they may have been an issue.

It was not clear how Ray and Janet had arrived at the sense of shared leadership in their marriage, but it was identified as a strength, perhaps even a form of solidarity between a man demonstrating healthy interdependence with an alternative culture and resilience in a dominant culture and a woman who was able to connect with an alternative family system across cultural difference. If this was an accurate interpretation of their respective capabilities, Ray and Janet brought many resources to their effort at resolving difficulties in their family. Janet referred to her family of origin as having been harmful to her, with what sounded like a "cutoff" at the point she married Ray. One wonders if this experience of outright rejection, interpreted as oppressive or unjust, resulted in the emergence of solidarity with Ray and his family. Janet's face brightened when she spoke of Ray's mother as a woman who was kind and generous, perhaps as a kind of role model for who Janet wanted to be in her own immediate family. If this assessment is accurate, it would exemplify the paradox of the power of rejection, or "cutoff," creating "counterpower" in the form of resistance and new connection, so that what appears to undermine or inhibit communal life fosters new and unpredicted connections.

Ray's concern that Janet would change if she went back to school and/or that others would evaluate their marriage as unequal in power with Janet as the "boss" was an important clarification of the problem they faced. Once he had given voice to this concern, and Janet heard it rather than the assumption that he perceived her as bossy or didn't want her to go back to school, she was able to empathize a bit more with the impact of her decision upon his interactions with his brothers. This clarification seemed to clear the way for them to reclaim their strength as partners to manage whatever evaluations might occur from Ray's brothers and to think more carefully about how they could build on their commitment to a kind of complementarity able to accommodate individual change in their marriage. One difference between Ray and Janet was their practice of faith. Janet attended worship on Sundays and read Scripture and prayed on a regular basis, while Ray, who was not interested in attending church, prayed "in his own way." This difference was not an issue they wanted to pursue in counseling. Their brief statements in the assessment form indicate it may not have been an issue at all. Janet expressed more concern about their children not participating in the life of the church than about Ray's disinterest.

At the end of the second session with Ray and Janet, the counselor attempted to extend the process in order to probe a bit more about Ray's concern that Janet would change if she went to school, to predict with them that change is inevitable for both of them, and to hear from each what changes they anticipated in themselves and each other. The caregiver felt that additional counseling would help them improve their communication, address the issue of "togetherness" in their family, as Janet had initially portrayed the problem, and pursue the counselor's own curiosity about how they managed difference and how shared leadership had emerged in their relationship. But Ray and Janet chose to conclude counseling at this point, and the counselor expressed appreciation to Ray for his willingness to participate in the second session.

Having used persuasion many times, now I try instead to stick with the problem as it is collaboratively understood with clients and to pose options for (1) continuing to work together to build on initial changes, (2) concluding counseling "at least for now," and (3) simply mutually agreeing on termination of the process. Sometimes a counselor's curiosity turns out *not* to be a mistake, and the counselor's encouragement to continue yields fruitful progress in additional growth or resolution of a problem. But due, in part, to the influence of feminist and narrative therapeutic theories, I am more cautious about such persuasion, especially with persons who are having difficulty asserting themselves or if pursuit of my research interests seems too important, relative to client benefit. Demonstrating respect for people whose goals for themselves are different or "less than" mine would be for them is crucial. Interpreting dynamics of power on the basis of theological criteria is crucial at this point in order for the caregiver to reflect God's justice and compassion and not overtake a careseeker's purpose. In my view, feminist therapeutic theories are particularly instructive as they inform proclamation as a purpose of caregiving, ideology as a value in feminist interpretation, and the consequences of dynamics of power in the caring relationship itself. When a caregiver facilitates the intersection of experience and tradition, drawing from diverse perspectives, new interpretations and more effective care are likely to emerge.

Consulting in Conflict and Difference

Fostering caring community is one interpretation of the purpose of an administrative type of pastoral consultation selected for purposes of this project because of its capacity to illustrate both interdependence and conflict in a specific dilemma as it occurred in a congregation. Other purposes of an administrative type of pastoral consultation include a training process for lay caregivers, more straightforward problem solving, clarification of identity and purpose of the congregation and development of programs congruent with this focus, or preparation for the future life of the church, sometimes including the call of a new pastor.

The consultant with whom First Community Church contracted was clear from the beginning that Donna would continue to play a key role in the future of the congregation and readily offered her support and encouragement for her efforts in continuing the outreach programs that were in place. The consultant also soon realized that the prospect of a small after-school program for children in the immediate neighborhood of the church was inhibited, in part, by the resistance of two members of the board to including a number of African American children in the congregation or inviting their parents to attend worship. As the consultant proceeded with interviewing members of the congregation in small groups, the issues of inclusivity and racism emerged as an implied but unspoken dividing line within the membership. The pastor had been outspoken on this matter on behalf of serving persons in need with the resources available, regardless of racial, economic, or religious difference.

Members of the congregation who had not previously voiced their opinions began to do so once the pastor had left. Sam, a member of the board who also served as the part-time janitor, and his daughter-in-law, who taught Sunday school and was also on the board, held the opinion that it was fine to help people with food and clothing but not invite "them" into "our" church. In one small group meeting, the consultant asked Sam what basis he had for this view, and Sam's reply was that the church didn't have the resources to meet all the needs of "these folks" and needed to pay attention to who was already in the pew. As the consultation process progressed, a proposal to begin an after-school program for neighborhood children was developed through Donna's leadership in cooperation with the two other congregations. The consultant recommended that the proposal not be put to a vote until it was clearer what the pastoral leadership of the church would be in the next year or so.

Donna and two other members of the board, however, felt that it would benefit the church to move forward with this project and were anticipating their involvement in caring for the children. The result of the board's vote was that the congregations would proceed with the after-school program. Sam and his daughter-in-law then submitted their resignations from the board and withdrew the memberships of the six adult members of their family. Despite several efforts by the consultant, Donna, and other members of the church encouraging Sam and his family members to reconsider, they did not return to the congregation. Within a year of this event, First Community Church and one of the other congregations in the ecumenical effort called a pastor to a three-quarter-time position, and the after-school program was underway with ten children participating on a regular basis.

Sam may have understood leaving First Community Church as separation from harm to that congregation, particularly if he viewed the church as set apart from, rather than within, its neighborhood. He may have demonstrated a kind of pragmatism if his concern about becoming more inclusive was based on his view of economic "reality" and on a fear that inviting families who did not appear to have the resources to help solve the financial difficulties of the church might add to, rather than alleviate, this problem. Had the opportunity existed, the consultant might have tried to help Sam distinguish between faithfulness to the history and identity of the congregation as he understood it and faithfulness to "living" tradition and to the living God, who calls forth newness in unpredictable ways.

Pastoral care beyond the therapeutic paradigm often conceptualizes problems and their resolution through a group process and draws from a systems view of a congregation in its context of local neighborhood and larger community. Survival is a major concern in many congregations and, in some, comes to dominate the time and energy of pastors and lay leaders. Viewing a congregation as one component of a wider community, vitally connected not only with the denomination of which it is a part but with the families and the immediate neighborhood in which it is located, may alter the sense of purpose and mission to which it is called. Gary Gunderson has portrayed the role of congregations in improving the quality of life and health in local communities in a move toward more "public" faithfulness on the part of these communities of faith.[7] When congregations view themselves as vital links between individuals, families, local communities, and larger sociocultural forces, the nature of the connections they make can effect a difference in many lives. As congregations identify their strengths, in addition to the knowledge they have developed about the difficulties they face, they may discover small but significant steps they can take in becoming more faithful in caring for persons in need.

The illustrations provided in this chapter have suggested the intersection of theological and therapeutic theory in understanding a variety of situations of pastoral care and have signaled the need for additional sources of knowledge beyond the therapeutic that will function as theories of continuity and change in pastoral ministry. In the concluding chapter, I will summarize the themes of the project and identify issues that warrant future exploration.

---

7. Gary Gunderson, *Deeply Woven Roots: Improving the Quality of Life in Your Community* (Minneapolis: Fortress Press, 1995), 19. Gunderson identifies eight strengths of congregations that enhance their role in a community, including strengths to accompany, convene, connect, give sanctuary, give context, bless, pray, and persist.

Chapter Five

Anticipatory Activity in Pastoral Ministry

Feminist revisions in pastoral care and counseling offer a partial but illuminating contribution to effective pastoral response in many situations of need. Recognizing the inextricable relation between the internal and external worlds and the integral relation of individual and communal experience, feminist revisions alter the relation of caregiver and careseeker in a collaborative process, shape problem definition to include wider sociocultural influence and contingencies, and view faithfulness in relation to God's activity. Employing a praxis method through which three themes emerged in the practice of ministry, I have engaged in an expanded version of pastoral theological reflection, exploring the sources of knowledge that inform, clarify, and alter pastoral response to need. Several theological viewpoints related to the themes have been explored in an effort to make explicit the theological assumptions operative in pastoral care, particularly an adequate understanding of God and our response and relation to God. Selected psychological and therapeutic theories have been discussed in order to explore theories of change and continuity in the helping process and to develop a more adequate "working" theory of self. I have suggested through several illustrations from practice of ministry how the themes of this project are clarified in some cases and exposed as ambiguous in others, influencing both theory and practice as a result.

Several issues have emerged around nurturing sufficient continuity and flexibility in a careseeker's identity and purpose in response to God, even as our partial representations of God are revised through diverse interpretation and experience. The freedom of God to call forth something apart from or outside a faith tradition and an individual's freedom to respond to that sense of call may be both creative and disruptive as varied notions of faithfulness emerge. Such revision may occur through the church's own proclamation of the gospel and unintended consequences among persons who have a different interpretation as they encounter God's Word. Revision may occur as the "historicity" of a particular viewpoint, such as a monarchical model of God's activity as domination and benevolence,

becomes clearer. The consequences of practice based on this representation of God have proved harmful, and alternatives based on Scripture,
tradition, and experience are emerging.

Resistance as an affirmation of agency and effective use of power can
itself be a form of faithfulness, particularly when it is shaped through
community so that this sign of vitality and resourcefulness is congruent
enough with the conditions and circumstances it seeks to redress. Self-
critical awareness of "gaps" between the inner promptings that may direct
resistance and the social influences perceived as harmful or oppressive
must be maintained so that the resistance fits the problem. If the personal
is political, it cuts both ways, and awareness that some rationalization or
distortion may occur in perceiving the source or conditions of harm will
increase the likelihood of resistance helping create conditions for justice
and anticipating liberation.

Naming interdependence in community as a desirable form of relationship suggests a shift in previous notions of leadership and a different
emphasis in one's understanding of the community formed through Jesus
Christ. I have used the term "connection," rather than simply "relationship," to connote not only interpersonal relationships but what may
appear to be more facile "givens." Individuals and families are related to or
"joined" with a myriad of institutions, social and ecological systems, and
cultural forces that exercise influence, which we are more conscious of
when they are problematic. The term "connection" also aptly includes the
"electronic" relationship that many have through global computer net-
works, new connections made on the basis of shared interests and access
to vast sources of information. The issue these connections create when
they become a source of harm or interference with other relationships or
commitments is becoming evident. The sense of the self as embodied in
the contingencies of physical and material reality and embedded in a web
of forceful influences has been prevalent in feminist thought.

One dimension of an adequate theory of self or theological anthropology is some sense of the continuity in subjective experience resulting from
the psychological patterns, or a psychic "structure," unique to the individual, patterns or structure that is amenable to change through enhanced
self-awareness and sometimes through therapeutic process. In addition to
individual subjectivity, agency, or the capacity to act, to influence, and to
exercise power as individuals and through communal efforts, is a second
dimension of theological anthropology. A third dimension is acknowledgment that our lives are communal and interdependent, a "web of
connections" that characterize our life in the force fields of God's world.

These three dimensions—subjectivity, agency, interdependence—are co-inherent, and not easily dichotomized or set in opposition as individual and communal, finite and eternal, psychological and social. In my view, feminist revisions are indeed thought experiments that attend to outcomes of practice, new ways of seeing that encourage altered understanding of ourselves and our place in God's world. Habitual as dualistic thinking is for many of us, finding constructs that help us move beyond dichotomous thinking can help us live with and even celebrate difference, some uncertainties, and partiality.

In concluding this project, I return to the notion of anticipatory activity as one way of identifying our purpose as caregivers and the practice of faith we are encouraging in careseekers. I will summarize the implications of this process of pastoral theological reflection in terms of anticipatory activity and conclude with suggestions for ongoing revisions in pastoral theology. Faithful response to God specifies the freedom we seek and the power we claim in the peculiar terms of God's own activities. Pastoral care, counseling, and consultation that try to reflect and anticipate, as much as possible, the compassion and justice of God may find criteria for practice of ministry through consideration of the link between what we do and what God may already be doing in any situation of care.

Faithfulness Reflecting and Anticipating Creation

In the original conceptualization of two themes of this project several years ago, I reflected on resistance and connection as they emerged in specific situations of pastoral care and counseling with both theological and therapeutic implications. In the years since that time, as I have continued to practice and teach pastoral theology and counseling, the additional theme of response to God took shape as a dilemma of purpose in the practice of ministry and what we are promoting through it. Three persistent questions led to the additional theme of faithful response to God: (1) What is the role of relation and response to God in helping persons to maintain coherent identity in the face of fragmenting forces or disruption in the continuity of their subjective experience? (2) How are God's agency and influence taken into account when caregiver and careseeker are exploring the relative influence of the problem upon the careseeker and, in turn, the influence careseekers may bring to bear upon the problem? (3) How is God related to the dynamics of power in community and portrayed without being reduced to a "functional resource," or misrepresented as unresponsive to particular suffering or ineffective in its alleviation?

These questions about God's relation to our subjectivity, agency, and interdependence emerged in many conversations with careseekers as we tried to account for God's presence and what God might be calling forth and to identify the careseeker's responsible, faithful action that might alleviate, or at least diminish, suffering. Through pastoral theological reflection, the distinct issue of relation and response to God emerged as a theme warranting discussion with careseekers in order to clarify their sense of God's activity or absence, their own responsibility (or sense of powerlessness) in relation to what God may be doing, and the ways in which this response and responsibility were shaped, limited, and specified through individual and communal commitments.

Living in response to God implies a relation of trust, a belief in the reliability of the one who is trusted based upon sufficient knowledge. Many situations of care involve calling such trust into question because God seems to be unreliable, breaking a pattern that was assumed to be fixed, or unpredictable, inviting change or choice that had not been imagined in the past. When caregivers are able to affirm predictable patterns in God's activity, as well as God's freedom to do something different than we expect, a way may be opened more accurately and fully to represent God through collaborative understanding. I have selected only three patterns in God's activity for discussion in the limits of this project, and surely many more have been suggested even in the brief theological explorations included here. But if caregivers are promoting response to God's activity in creation and re-creation, how would caregiving be revised as a result?

Letty Russell's notion of partnership toward the new creation is helpful in identifying how a careseeker and caregiver might interpret their respective purposes in alignment with and response to God's creativity. If the collaborative perception is that God is causing something new to come into being by resisting what has been, constructing a different outcome than had been expected, or designing a revised version of a previously coherent identity, then naming this as God's creativity at work can make a difference. Even briefly calling some representation of God to the forefront of dialogue in pastoral care may alter the context, process, purpose, and outcome. Two theological affirmations from my denomination's interpretation of the Reformed theological tradition are the sovereignty of God and the rediscovery of God's grace in Jesus Christ, revealed through Scripture. Understood as an attribute of God sometimes linked with a distant, absolute power, above and independent from the world, *sovereignty* is one among many issues in theology that have received repeated attention and critique among feminist theologians, including those cited in this project. When connected more fully with the grace of God known through the incarnation, the attribution of power is not unproblematic but does point toward a different use of power and demonstrates the freedom of God.

In my encounters with caregivers over the years, I have discussed God's grace a great deal more than I have divine sovereignty, in part because of the feminist critique of this patriarchal, hierarchical notion of power. While I am sympathetic with the purposes of Sallie McFague's revision in a more "panentheistic" model of creation—the world as God's body— the freedom of God portrayed in more fully "trinitarian" understandings of creation and re-creation is more accurate to scriptural representations and, in my view, more helpful in distinguishing between and connecting our activity and that of God.[1] Emphasizing God's freedom to act, to bring something out of nothing, making interdependence an integral part of creation and declaring it good—these are open to distortion, especially when transcendent power is disconnected from the consequences of grace. Pastoral care that tries to reflect creation and anticipate new creation may participate in the distortion of God's transcendence as a kind of tyranny, even terrorism, if it fails to contradict the harm done by those who invoke God to justify their misuse of power. Feminist theological revisions that emphasize and foster imagination of intimate relation with God, God's parental, passionate, and companionable love for and involvement with all of creation, have broadened my conceptualization of and language for God's relation to the world in a manner that is constructive. The range of representations for God encountered in pastoral ministry calls for broadened imagination as well as recognition of what is missing or unspoken as careseekers give voice to their sense of how God views

---

1. Daniel L. Migliore, *Faith Seeking Understanding: An Introduction to Christian Theology* (Grand Rapids: Eerdmans, 1991), 92–95. Migliore defines three understandings of the relationship between God and the world in this way: "Theism is the belief that God is the transcendent creator of the world, pantheism is the belief that the world is a mode of God's being, and panentheism is the belief that the world and God are mutually dependent." Migliore goes on to say that none of these understandings is adequate to a trinitarian doctrine of God and creation. Migliore critiques the panentheistic model exemplified in McFague's work as expressing the intimacy and reciprocity of the relationship between God and the world but "incapable of articulating the gracious, nonnecessary, asymmetrical relationship of God to the world described in the Bible." Ibid., 93.

their situation or how God is thought to be present or absent in relation to a problem.

Representing God's power in imminent, intimate, relational terms enables careseekers to take sufficient responsibility for the influence they do have in addressing a problem. Feminist theology is particularly helpful in a selective and compensatory portrayal of God's power through the incarnation and in our power to be helpful through partnership toward the new creation. Representing God's power as freedom to re-create, departing from previous patterns on which the person had relied yet inviting trust in God's benevolent and gracious use of power, is an accurate and effective reflection and anticipation of what God may be doing. Representing God's power or suggesting that God is actively present at all may be a notable statement of faith, even an act of resistance, in a postmodern world. McFague discusses a deconstructionist view of desire for God's presence as childish nostalgia, though she does not share this view:

> The desire for full presence, whether in the form of nostalgia for the garden of Eden, or the quest for the historical Jesus, or the myth of God incarnate, is [in the deconstructionist view] a denial of what we know as adults to be the case in human existence: such innocence, certainty, and absoluteness are not possible. What deconstruction, with its denial of all presence, brings out powerfully is that absence is even more prevalent than presence: the world in which we live is one in which we create structures to protect us against the chaos, absence, death, oppression, and exclusion that surround us.[2]

The deconstructionist viewpoint considered in McFague's work functions as some feminist viewpoints have in my own: calling into question operative theological assumptions and inviting or requiring clarification in response. McFague suggests that the deconstructionist critique requires "negative capability," or the ability "to endure absence, uncertainty, partiality, relativity, and to hold at bay the desire for closure, coherence, identity, totality."[3] Deconstructionism stops short of identifying what

---

2. Sallie McFague, *Models of God: Theology for an Ecological, Nuclear Age* (Philadelphia: Fortress Press, 1987), 25. McFague views the deconstructionist critique, beginning with Friedrich Nietzsche, as a perceptive critique of Western metaphysics, insisting that there is nothing but metaphor: "Deconstruction concludes that the root metaphor of human existence is writing and interprets writing literally as metaphoricity itself." Ibid., 23. For an introduction to deconstructionist thought, see Christopher Norris, *Deconstruction: Theory and Practice* (London: Methuen, 1982).

3. McFague, *Models of God*, 25.

constructions or reconstructions would be helpful, as McFague notes in her own project of a constructive revisioning of theology. She maintains that her own constructive efforts are better for our time than constructions that ignore the context of "a holistic vision and the nuclear threat" in which we live.

As I have "lived in the house" of resistance and connection as anticipatory activity, dwelling with these constructions for several years while teaching and practicing pastoral theology and counseling, the question of faithfulness, and to what or to whom, has emerged again and again. Trust in God's presence is not often absolute, and faith that God acts on our behalf may be tentative, shaken, uncertain in the midst of suffering. In a manner of speaking, people who seek pastoral care have been through "deconstruction" of sorts and need someone to dwell there with them as they reconstruct and are re-created. The capacity to live with ambiguity, long thought to be a hallmark of maturity, means, not giving up faith, but learning to live with "the desire for closure, coherence, identity, totality," even when it is unfulfilled. The "not knowing" position now common for therapists influenced by social-constructionist thought has given way in pastoral care and counseling to "appropriate knowing," meaning that it is possible to represent a faith perspective, to hear and privilege another's view, and to work together in understanding what relation faith may have to the problem or need being addressed.

Reflecting and anticipating creation through pastoral ministry mean that we neither overestimate nor underestimate the significance of our own and others' efforts to be faithful. The value of considering this "location" of our actions relative to God's actions is to encourage creative activity, to identify some criteria for discerning what it will be as it corresponds to our knowledge of God's creativity and purpose. As Clive reconsidered his place in the larger scheme of things, perhaps God was calling Clive to some knowledge of God's sovereignty in relation to creation and to new and difficult recognition of his own mortality as "creature." Such knowledge of our identity and purpose in relation to God in response to crisis, especially life-threatening crisis, is common ground in pastoral care. The difference that feminist thought may make in these encounters with careseekers in crisis is in the understanding of God. Representing God as sovereign and gracious, to use the terms of a Reformed view, or as parental, passionate, companionable, and the like, to use more relational terms, opens space for a diversity of faithful, creative responses.

Resistance as Anticipatory Liberation

As aspects of God's activity in relation to humanity and all creation, liberation and reconciliation are integrally related. However, liberation is distinct from reconciliation in that it suggests a process or history in which persons are set free or delivered from oppression or bondage. Reconciliation, on the other hand, is understood as the purpose of the history of liberation and as the event through which liberation is realized in Jesus Christ, when people are given new and joyful life in relation to one another and to God.[4] In the praxis method of this project, the process of liberation has been explored in relation to a selected activity of resistance to harm and oppression. I have suggested that struggles for freedom are characterized by creative forms of resistance that may appear to thwart a goal or purpose of reconciliation with God and other persons.

The preceding discussion of resistance has indicated that such behavior may actually be a more creative and less defensive means for moving toward a goal or anticipating a vision of the "good" because it draws on a particular, historical situation as well as the inner promptings within an individual. Our efforts on behalf of liberation, including encouraging acts of creative, appropriate resistance, are determined by the particular conditions and circumstances of bondage or sin as well as by the purpose of reconciliation. Pastoral care is understood in this way as a ministry of Jesus Christ in which God's history of liberation and the event of reconciliation in Jesus Christ are remembered and in which God's future liberation and reconciliation are actively anticipated.

The themes of resistance and connection that I have explored through feminist theology and theory offered a way to make sense of the experiences of some persons I have tried to help. But in suggesting that creative resistance may be understood as anticipating liberation and that interdependent connections may be interpreted as anticipating reconciliation, I have developed a particular interpretation of experience. This selected rhetorical strategy emerged from both ideological and theo-

---

4. Reconciliation was the central theological theme of the Confession of 1967 of the Presbyterian Church (U.S.A.). For many years as a pastor teaching new member classes, I discussed this confession particularly on the subject of reconciliation in society and how God's love overcomes barriers of racism and other forms of discrimination. It has become clearer that a call for reconciliation means working on both relational and material conditions for justice. See *The Constitution of the Presbyterian Church (U.S.A.)*, part 1, *Book of Confessions* (Louisville: Office of the General Assembly, Presbyterian Church (U.S.A.), 1996), 259–70.

logical perspectives that "made sense" of experience by focusing on possibilities for action in the present in light of expectations for God's future and our own. Actions that help create the conditions for freedom from bondage or liberation from oppression occur within connections and relationships of interdependence. Appropriate resistance may mean respect for courage and endurance in circumstances of oppression that will not change quickly, realizing that such regard or empathy may itself change the conditions of suffering. These actions to enhance freedom occur in relationships of interdependence in which power is misused, misdirected, or denied and in which joy and reconciliation would be signs of new creation, but reconciliation on our preferred terms is not always possible.

Resistance may involve challenge to structural evil or particular configurations of power and knowledge. Resistance may mean separating oneself from a harmful person or situation in order to be safe and prevent further harm. It may mean redirecting one's energies or revising one's goals rather than continuing to thwart a self-established goal. Resistance may also mean changing a pattern of thought or habitual behavior that has resulted from internalized oppression. It may involve a group's support and encouragement of an individual engaged in self-reliant, self-affirming actions within a system. Resistance may include a group's action to alleviate suffering caused by misuse of power. Resistance may mean withstanding or enduring a force or influence that is harmful or refraining from a response with forbearance in order to avoid further harm.

One woman with whom I worked in a pastoral counseling relationship was separated from her husband, who had engaged in several affairs during their marriage. As the woman moved through the difficult passage toward divorce, we talked about this step as a kind of resistance to further erosion of her self-respect and emotional vitality and about the connections she was nurturing with a few friends and family as resistance to isolation, her initial temptation. As a woman of steady faith, she seemed to trust her future, and her husband's, with God, and continued to pray for him. Although the divorce was certainly a signal of disconnection, this careseeker engaged in activity, including prayer, that anticipated reconciliation, which God would grant, she believed, not in the form of repairing her marriage, but in "saving" her husband from a form of unfaithfulness that she had been unable to influence.[5]

---

5. In numerous situations of care and counseling, I have drawn from an interpretation of reconciliation offered by J. Randall Nichols in a discussion of ministry with

A specifically theological notion of liberation from harm or oppression as a condition for reconciliation may disclose particular meanings in experience, evoking different possibilities for action and in that way more fully directing a process of pastoral counseling. A caregiver or counselor who locates a person's experience in the context of God's creative and redemptive activity—explicitly understood as action anticipating liberation and reconciliation—may discern alternative theological understandings which will evoke anticipatory freedom for some.

Liberation is a primary biblical and theological theme, an experience of what God has done in history and in the event of Jesus Christ, and this crucial emphasis is becoming more fully integrated in pastoral care and counseling. Feminist and liberation theological perspectives help to construct a practice of ministry that integrates a theme of liberation when it is appropriate to do so. Deideologization and remythologizing of Scripture and feminist revisions of theology have enabled a clearer understanding of God's initiative and action to set persons free in order that we may love and serve one another and may tend, rather than dominate or destroy, creation. Developing a liberative perspective in pastoral care does not displace other understandings of this form of ministry, but it does alter the response to a person's need, shape problems and solutions in a new way, and reflect a fuller understanding of God's initiative in the history of faith.

Without attention to this aspect of God's activity and our ministry in response, we are less likely to care for persons in ways that fit the context, and more likely to miss the structured relations of sin and suffering. In some situations, the need for liberation and the possibilities for creative resistance in order to enhance freedom are conditions for and must occur prior to efforts that anticipate reconciliation. Creative resistance and conflict are sometimes a prelude to healthier connection and community

---

the divorced. Nichols analyzed the myth of the "friendly divorce" and distinguished between civility and friendship as, respectively, a code of interaction and a relationship. He argues that civility may or may not lead to friendship but that "it is only when boundaries are clear and adequately protected that neighborliness flourishes." Nichols suggests that sometimes reconciliation in divorce means "putting an end to mutual destructiveness and hostility" so that personal boundaries are recontracted and the two parties are free to go their separate ways in peace. This seems to suggest that in some instances divorce may be the most desirable "connection." See J. Randall Nichols, "Rethinking Some Aspects of Ministry to the Divorced: A Theological Retake," *Journal of Pastoral Care* 42, no. 2 (summer 1988): 101–15. For purposes of this project, I have maintained the notion of healthy connection as anticipating reconciliation in order to clarify that reconciliation is something that God accomplishes.

and may, for the time being, constitute the only way in which a person can anticipate either liberation or its further purpose of reconciliation. My experience in leading a women's issues group in an agency setting provided an opportunity to hear from the women how they viewed the interrelation of intrapsychic, physiological, interpersonal, family, and contextual influences in their lives. Each had particular understandings of God and their relation to God, of what this meant for their relationships with others, of their practice of faith and participation in the church. The women emphasized the harm done to them in oppressive relationships and what needed to change, or their personal responsibility for their own suffering and what they and the other person needed to change.

One of the women, who was separated from her husband due to the consequences of his alcoholism, continued to have contact with him, which perpetuated mutual harm in the form of verbal abuse and threats. In this instance, marital separation was not a form of creative resistance to harm or a process of liberation from the oppression of the relationship or the bondage of alcoholism. In a sense, neither resistance nor liberation was possible in this problematic connection because the woman was insistent upon marital reconciliation and firm in her belief that this was God's will, though she knew the effects of the relationship contradicted other aspects of what she identified as God's will—that she not feel like a failure. I had encouraged her to use her anger as vital information about what needed to change and as energy for a constructive purpose, a potential resistance to misuse of power. But dwelling with her resistance to change, as we did for a few months in the counseling process, was intended to disclose more understanding of something in her situation and its structures, or within herself, that would suggest possibilities we hadn't considered. If resistance had been discussed in this situation in more explicit terms of anticipating liberation and in light of God's freedom to do something new and unpredicted, perhaps this situation would have been more carefully located within God's activity and purpose. Although I do not know whether this would have made a difference, such a rhetorical, or theological, "strategy" based on "faith-knowledge" of God might have altered the helping process.

The notion that a gap in congruence between a situation and a person's response to it indicates some form of resistance is useful, provided the incongruity is valued as important information about both the person and the situation. This understanding of resistance suggests that, like Ray in relation to his boss (although this was not the focus of the counseling process), someone who remains in a difficult or harmful situation may be responding to aspects of that situation of which the counselor is not yet aware or to inner meaning or distortion that needs to be explored in order to be understood. Such inner meaning might reflect a sense of commitment to relationship on account of the covenant of marriage, or a commitment to provide for one's family, or a desire to continue trying to help a partner who is in need. In many such instances, resistance may appear to be avoidance of change, but it may also be an alternative to despair or hopelessness. If it results in increasing suffering and perpetuates harm, it becomes clearer that this is probably not endurance on behalf of or in anticipation of liberation or reconciliation. However, the vitality and resourcefulness disclosed in such resistance can be valued and, perhaps, redirected in a process of care or counseling.

In my review of feminist theological perspectives, I identified a number of differences I have with the views of Sallie McFague, Sharon Welch, and Rita Nakashima Brock. These differences are apparent in my work with careseekers who are revising their own understanding of God as distinct from a tradition's representation of God. A sense of God's freedom "from" and "for" the world, a faith tradition, or any group or individual is one way of thinking about divine sovereignty and grace that encourages our persistence and freedom in the face of limitations and failures. On the other hand, it is in human relationship in a context of care and counseling that space and time are granted in order to be free to work through painful issues, to give up defenses that do not fit the person or the situation any longer, to make distinctions and identify commonalities in such a way that forgiveness and integrity are more possible. In a sense this corresponds with feminist "immanental" theology in which human relationships are sufficient for healing, particularly if a theological perspective is not so much explained with authority in order to define someone's experience as discerned after accurately and empathically understanding the meanings in another's experience. The significant contribution of these feminist theological perspectives is in their insistence upon practice as a criterion of truth and the affirmation that God is concerned with the material, historical particularity of our lives.

Connection as Anticipatory Reconciliation

Several issues in feminist revisions of Christology have emerged through this process of pastoral theological reflection on practice of ministry. Feminist theology and psychotherapy have turned toward an emphasis on community and communal relationships and the ways in which individuals are shaped and influenced by social interaction and cultural systems. The turn toward the importance of relationality or interconnection de-emphasizes a focus on individuals and individual existential experience so that the broader picture of the social, political, economic, and eco-logical context can be considered. This shift in scope is understood to be for the sake of the survival of creation and is articulated in more recent works in feminist theology, including McFague's discussion of the world as God's body.

The argument of this project has been largely in support of the shift to-ward emphasizing community and has valued attention to relationship in community, including that found between careseekers and caregiver. The emergence of systems theory and its use in congregations and groups and with families has offered invaluable means for understanding and helping to address problems in a broad range of systems impinging on pastoral care situations. However, I have chosen to address a specific issue related to this turn toward relationality—the question of what it requires on the part of individuals to live faithfully in community. Using a praxis method, I have argued that it requires capacities for creativity to imagine how things could be different and readiness for change, for appropriate resistance congruent enough with the situation and the inner promptings of individuals, and for interdependent connections in which some capacity exists for empa-thy or understanding the experience of another who is different from oneself.

Connection connotes a relationship in which there is an intervening link or bond that forms an affinity or alliance between the persons or person and system. I have chosen not to use the word "community" to identify this relation because it is commonly used in feminist theology in a way that seems to diminish individual difference and agency. The term "connection" is certainly subject to the same peril but offers the possibil-ity of analyzing the intervening "link" that forms the connection. This theme has also been useful because it may avoid the sense of absorption or opposition in the relation between individual and community. A care-giver is interested in disclosing and nurturing forms of community in which people are sufficiently connected and affiliated and in which affir-mation of individual agency and self-reliance also occur. Oppression or suffering cannot be the only defining feature of community membership if initiatives toward freedom and health are to be enhanced.

Recall the example of the peer support gatherings with single-parent women. The group worked by connecting and networking to offer strate-gies in addressing problems in the systems with which they were required to interact. Individuals were free to ask for attention to urgent, specific needs, which may or may not have reflected issues the women held in common. This illustration portrays women connecting in collective efforts to work on systemic causes of problems they share and to work with one another in their respective efforts toward healthier lives, without assuming that those two efforts are always the same or can be accomplished in the same way. In the discussion of interdependence and how Jesus Christ makes community possible, I tried not to set up a false opposition between individual and communal and not to suggest that individualism is necessarily anticommunal.[6]

On the contrary, God's work of reconciliation in Jesus Christ creates community by enabling individuals to be together and, generally speaking, to work toward a common purpose. Reconciliation is an understanding of what God was doing in Jesus Christ according to the biblical witness and theological interpretations of that witness. Reconciliation is a primary function of pastoral ministry as people are enabled more fully to receive and respond to God's grace and forgiveness, to appropriate the transforming gift of faith, and to be healed and restored in such a way that love and service are possible.

Knowledge about the historical Jesus as well as theological assertions about the meaning of his life, death, and resurrection help to distinguish among ideological understandings of Jesus Christ and make it more difficult to interpret him only as a reflection of particular human needs. In this way, it becomes clearer that Jesus Christ bears meaning for ideological concerns and purposes but always transcends or moves beyond them as well. In the praxis method I have used, a better balance in understanding the creative, reconciling, and liberating activity of God in Jesus Christ is called for in order to respond to human suffering. Liberation does not fully displace reconciliation as a way to understand God's action and our calling, but actions that anticipate liberation may be necessary before justice in interdependent relationships is possible.

I have argued that oppression as an identifying experience for a group of persons may have the effect of emphasizing powerlessness at the expense of possibility. Sam viewed the African American families to whom

---

6. For a full discussion of Emersonian individualism and self-reliance, see Donald Capps, *The Depleted Self: Sin in a Narcissistic Age* (Minneapolis: Fortress Press, 1993). Capps defends an ideology of individualism against contemporary scapegoating and views individualists as those seeking truer forms of community than existing institutions (including churches) provide.

the congregation was reaching out, and whose children would be invited to the ecumenical after-school program, as oppressed and in need, and he was willing for the church to offer assistance through food and clothing. However, Sam's categorization of these families on the basis of race and economic status led to a kind of refusal of relationship in community, a refusal of diversity and interdependence as members of a faith community, in which he would come to know and rely upon them in their efforts as participants in community.

The illustrations in this project have demonstrated some of the difficulty in introducing more systemic, political perspectives on issues careseekers face. Liberation and feminist perspectives are needed in order to avoid the hazards of reinforcing the power arrangements of patriarchy as they are played out in biased views of race and ethnicity, economic class, and other categories of experience.[7] And yet I view this as a theological issue, claiming that Jesus Christ makes different human relationship possible because he serves to contradict and correct our biases and mistakes, intentional or otherwise. In this way, community established on account of God's relationship with us in creation and incarnation continues to attempt clearer reflection of the person and work of Jesus Christ, knowing that human community alone will never complete "the" new creation. Feminist revisions encourage the church and its representatives who are caregivers to be faithful in proclamation and practice based on diverse experiences, living tradition in a variety of contexts, and multiple interpretations of Scripture that sufficiently correspond to the history of interpretation and yet are credible across a range of differences and situations of need. In this way, revisions support practices of faith including "criticizing and resisting all those powers and patterns that destroy human beings, corrode human community, and injure God's creation."[8]

Part of the task of pastoral ministry is to invite people to faith or a rediscovery of faith and a personal relationship with God through Jesus

---

7. Elisabeth Schüssler Fiorenza has used the term "kyriarchal" rather than "patriarchal" because the latter focuses on problems in terms of gender difference, implying that all men dominate all women, which is not the case. Her analysis suggests that the power arrangements of patriarchy as problematic in the project may need to be revised in terms that do not misconstrue oppression only in terms of gender. *Jesus—Miriam's Child, Sophia's Prophet: Critical Issues in Feminist Christology* (New York: Continuum, 1995), 12–18.

8. Theology and Worship Ministry Unit, Presbyterian Church (U.S.A.), *Growing in the Life of Christian Faith* (Louisville: Presbyterian Church (U.S.A.), Distribution Management Services, 1989), 28.

Christ. One cannot abandon attention to the second person of the Trinity as he is known to us through Scripture and by the work of God's Spirit through faith. At the same time, a tendency to privatize such faith may be especially strong in the context of pastoral care, where faith is viewed solely as a means for replenishing or nurturing one's self. If such privatization of faith and instrumental interpretation of its purpose conform to power arrangements that are oppressive, the systemic or structural dimensions of sin or suffering may remain unidentified, and connections with God's liberative activity in all of creation may remain obscured. As I see it, a fuller theological understanding of Jesus Christ and the origins of Christian faith can be based primarily on Scripture and the work of God's Spirit but also on the various and sometimes contradictory notions of the historical Jesus and the earliest Christian movement. Holding the individual and the community in integral connection fosters a fuller sense of faith's origins and present purpose.[9]

Feminist theories of psychology and therapy that focus on differences based on gender (those of Carol Gilligan and the Stone Center, for instance) seem to be the least compatible with the theological theme of liberation. In the process of this project, it has become clearer that at least some of the feminist theories that attempt identification of women's unique capacities do not acknowledge their foundations in prior theories, which were not gender specific. A different perspective on women's relational capacity has been integrated into care and counseling processes in which I have discussed partnership and interdependence as desirable, rather than promoting the notion of women having unique or superior relational capability.[10] Gilligan's theory of women's resistance to discon-

---

9. In addition to Brock's turn from the individual Jesus toward an emphasis on the community that surrounded and "co-created" him, noted works by Elisabeth Schüssler Fiorenza have reconstructed "a hermeneutical space for the ekklesia of wo/men" (*Jesus—Miriam's Child, Sophia's Prophet*, 30) in the earliest Jesus movement in order to articulate an alternative in the radical democracy, which she contends characterized this early community of disciples. In her latest work, Fiorenza argues that the construct or image of Jesus as Lord and Savior, even as revisioned in some feminist Christologies, is deeply embedded in contemporary religious and political processes of domination. Because of the pressing needs for liberation within our own global village, Fiorenza chooses a particular hermeneutical approach—a critical feminist theology of liberation—in order to analyze the effects of christological articulations in the lives of women.

10. A very helpful discussion of relationality may be found in Christie Cozad Neuger, "Women and Relationality," in *Feminist and Womanist Pastoral Theology*, ed. Bonnie Miller-McLemore and Brita Gill-Austern (Nashville: Abingdon, 1999),

nection values relationships as a context for development and growth and can, I believe, be extended to describe experiences of men encountered in pastoral care to identify the strength of their capacity and desire for connection.

When Clive described his experience of closeness with Gloria, his sense of being understood in their relationship, and his efforts to become available to his children in a way he hadn't been before, a growing ability for empathic connections and acknowledgment of interdependence signaled significant growth and change. As Janet heard more clearly Ray's concern about his family's perceptions of their relationship, a relationship already characterized by interdependence was strengthened as one partner was more able to imagine and respond to the experience of the other. In my view, theirs was an anticipation of the kind of reconciliation God desires and provides.

To the extent that Sam disclosed his concerns about moving forward with the after-school program, the other board members tried to understand and respond to his concern. Following his resignation, they attempted to "reconnect" with Sam and his family in order to restore the relationship that had been broken. Sam and his family chose not to accept this invitation, resisting the reconciling efforts of their longtime friends and coworkers at the church. It was as if Sam took himself out of relationship for the sake of maintaining his connection with the community as it had been, unable to remain in the community as it changed, and sought to be faithful in its altered context. As the community of faith moved forward with its outreach efforts, identified as broadening their caring community, anticipatory activity, glimmerings of solidarity, perhaps even small signs of the new creation, appeared at First Community Church. At the same time, it is a community that witnessed brokenness as well as sacredness, and in seeking to be inclusive, a few people in the community excluded themselves from participation. Expecting that God will restore and repair what has been broken, even in ways that we never see or comprehend, is not, in my view, childish nostalgia or utopian dream but bears witness to a kind of reconciliation that God has promised to provide.

113–33. Neuger identifies three key dimensions of feminist pastoral theology: (1) women's relationality as uniquely gendered; (2) the just and mutually enhancing ordering of relationships; and (3) theological understandings of relationship in the web of creation. She turns to a "historicist" alternative in order to talk about women's experience in a particular context and commends a relationality that "seeks out difference in order to celebrate it rather than look for one's self in the other." Ibid., 129.

Valuing "inherent" capacities for interdependent relationship or empathy based on gender is hazardous for pastoral care when it presumes a complementarity in relationships that may not be accurate. Frequently careseekers are not in situations in which income earning, household chores, and child care are shared tasks. Theories that emphasize gender difference have a tendency to obscure the complexity of social and material relations as if a person occupies one part of a complementary relationship or lives in social and economic structures that require gender-specific capability. The result may be reinforcement of gender-specific social relations that do not account for or encourage a spectrum of possibilities, including categories of identification other than gender. Working with Ray and Janet to increase the flexibility of their shared leadership in the family as well as encouraging their ability to accommodate one another as each changes and grows moves away from gender stereotypes and contradicts social forces (including Ray's brothers) who would find such accommodation unacceptable in marriage.

The notion of interdependent connection becomes problematic when used to describe relationship with God. Feminist theologies vary in their description of the God-world relationship, as mentioned in the earlier typology of theism, pantheism, and panentheism, the first characterizing the Reformed tradition as interpreted by my own denomination and the latter characterizing McFague's work. I have chosen to separate the theme of response to God, in part, to draw distinctions among (1) the interdependence that characterizes our relationship with other persons and all of creation, (2) our relation to God as one of dependence and agency, and (3) God's relation to us as influenced and affected by, but not entirely dependent upon, what we do. Feminist revisions challenge and broaden our capacity to respond to diverse representations of God and the God-world relation and to make choices in our inevitably selective nurturing of response to God among careseekers. In my view, we live in anticipation of joy and reconciliation in our relationships with God, with one another, and with creation. Appropriate forms of connection enable us to suffer with others and to empathize as we discern difference and likeness. Appropriate forms of connection include delight in and enjoyment of God as Creator, Savior, and sustaining Spirit, of one another in our diversity and commonality, and of creation entrusted to our care.

With this kind of expectation in mind, actions that respect and seek to understand difference, efforts toward more equitable and responsible use of power, empathy that intentionally listens for and resonates with another's thoughts and feelings, that does not turn away from pain, hospitality that fosters and celebrates friendship, intimacy that is resilient and tender, that endures and deepens through conflict, loss, daily pleasures, and play—these are joyful forms of connection that reflect and anticipate reconciliation in Jesus Christ. These forms of connection are anticipatory, preliminary, exercising power and agency in expectation of reconciliation, knowing that we are called to use what freedom we have in this way. God may choose to use what we do for purposes of new creation, liberation, and reconciliation, but God's activity is always also more than and beyond our efforts or the future we are able to imagine.

Ongoing Revisions in Pastoral Theology

In concluding this discussion of the contribution of feminist perspectives in pastoral care and counseling, I will summarize and specify the implications of more adequate attention to praxis and pastoral theological reflection. The consequences of identifying my theological "location" or viewpoint within the Reformed tradition was intended to serve the purpose of rendering more explicit some of the theological assumptions I brought to this effort. In doing so, my hope is that other equally valid viewpoints are more readily apparent by comparison and that further exploration will be prompted in others who reflect on a particular practice of ministry.

As stated early in this discussion, I have been challenged by dilemmas encountered in the experiences of careseekers to whom I have tried to respond and by engagement with a variety of theologies and psychological and therapeutic theories as I have tried to strengthen that response. The relation between experience and faith tradition, understood through thematic interpretation, has suggested a "link" between a caregiver's collaborative naming of the careseeker's experience and a partial but appropriate interpretation of tradition. I have chosen to extend feminist theory based upon women's experience to interpret problematic situations encountered by women and men, a choice based on the conviction that feminist perspectives are helpful to all provided they maintain regard and respect for difference and particularity of experience. Strategies of interpretation that focus on oppression or difference based on gender are not mutually exclusive, and yet the hazards of overemphasizing oppression (exacerbating powerlessness) or difference (suggesting dichotomous, opposite relation) often work against increasing freedom or nurturing relationship. For the purposes of pastoral ministry, it is crucial to maintain a fuller sense of the ambiguity and complexity of human experience even as we attempt clearer understanding and more helpful response.

Feminist theories have not developed a singular understanding of the self and have explored the social and cultural influences upon formation of the self and an "embedded" quality resulting from internalization of these forces. From a theological perspective, a defining sense of self is given in relation to God, and the purpose of the self is known through faith in Jesus Christ as guided by God's Spirit. But if power is inter-structured as thoroughly as feminist analysis suggests, then the heart of patriarchy is in some way my heart too, and I am called to explore my intermixing of both resistance and commitment to self-knowledge and to participate in the interconnections and community that God calls into being.

I have claimed that human activity—theologically understood—anticipates a different future and a new creation. Our practice of faith does not bring about God's future or constitute a kind of "natural progression" toward a new creation. But we are called to proclaim and practice faith in ways that anticipate the future as we know it in the life, death, and resurrection of Jesus Christ. I have suggested that particular forms of response to God, resistance to harm, and interdependent connections are more faithful and are signs of freedom and vitality, reflecting and anticipating God's presence and activity. I have discussed a kind of responsiveness in which a careseeker's sense of what God may be calling forth, clarified in conversation with a caregiver, shapes the responsible action to be taken in addressing a problem. Appropriate resistance to the structured dynamics of power can be an expression of solidarity with others who suffer in the same or similar circumstance, and new, unpredicted community may emerge as a result.

While a singular basis for the emergence of such solidarity and community may prompt its beginning, the tolerance, invitation, and even celebration of difference within community, hearing diverse expressions of what was thought to be common experience, can strengthen and help to sustain efforts to alleviate suffering. This means, in part, that neither political, social, or psychological forms of bondage or oppression offer the primary basis of our identity or an adequate explanation of suffering and sin. Interpretations that widen the lens, theorizing on the basis of diverse experience and broadening explanatory theory in several dimensions of experience, contribute to more accurate and effective helping relationships. Desirable forms of connection are characterized by interdependence with regard for "otherness," as we come to understand and empathize with the suffering of others and to enjoy and delight in our differences and commonalities. The multiple values of coherence and integrity of the self, as well as awareness of the contingency, partiality, and need for flexibility in identity, better serve caregivers' efforts to help others express and make sense of subjective experience.

Liberation and feminist theologies have been a focus of this effort in participating in revisions in pastoral care and counseling. The biblical and theological stream of liberation is a necessary but partial understanding of God's activity. The themes of this project have been connected to God's activity in re-creating, liberating, and reconciling and are, respectively, suggestive of the origin, process, and goal of God's relation to us and our efforts in pastoral ministry as response to God. The relational themes of response, resistance, and connection are three among many recurring yet partial dynamics in the experiences of careseekers that warrant pastoral theological reflection as part of a praxis method. Like themes in a musical composition, they have been identified more as short melodies, or a brief line of notes constituting a small part of one composition among a multitude of songs. And yet they are, at least for the time being, sufficiently recurrent in the lives of persons seeking pastoral care that further understanding is needed. As interpretive strategies, they enable an intersection of theological and therapeutic viewpoints useful for pastoral theologians and caregivers alike.

Five sources of knowledge for pastoral theological reflection were identified as practice of ministry, the social location and personhood of the caregiver or pastoral theologian, social or cultural/political theory that explains the context for ministry, the religious tradition in its formal and operational dimensions, and the supporting disciplines of psychology and psychotherapy. One of the most challenging aspects of the task of a pastoral theologian is conceptualizing the relationship among these sources, and a praxis method has guided this discussion. Theological criteria have been used to determine desirable forms and expressions of response to God, resistance, and connection.

At the intersection of the sources of knowledge, theories based upon women's experience magnify some aspects of experience and may distort other concerns. In particular, the interrelatedness and commonalities in women and men's experiences may not be identified through use of feminist perspectives. This suggests that feminist viewpoints can be expected to reveal aspects of commonality in oppression, or differences from men, and that it is crucial in pastoral care and counseling to anticipate the contradictions or exceptions to this viewpoint so that diversity of experience is heard and understood. As rhetorical strategy, interpretation of experience may be like persuasion, using language with acute awareness of its "productive" capability, sometimes helping to construct a different future through alternative interpretations of the past and present.

A praxis-oriented method involves selected sources of knowledge and interpretive strategies that shape pastoral theology as a "performative" theological discipline. As I have identified the links between our response and God's creativity, between acts of resistance and God's liberative power, and between interdependent connections and God's purpose of reconciliation, I have shown how theological meanings may direct efforts in pastoral ministry based on a specifically Christian vision of the future and call to faithfulness in the present. This vision is not based upon ideology alone, but our seeing is enhanced by the use of critical and constructive feminist perspectives.

Index

(i) Other books in the Introductions in Feminist Theology Series

INTRODUCING AFRICAN WOMEN'S THEOLOGY
MERCY AMBA ODUYOYE

Mercy Amba Oduyoye describes the context and methodology of Christian theology by Africans in the past two decades, offering brief descriptions and sample treatments of theological issues such as creation, Christology, ecclesiology, and eschatology. The daily spiritual life of African Christian women is evident as the reader is led to the sources of African women's Christian theology. This book reflects how African culture and its multi-religious context has influenced women's selection of theological issues.

ISBN 0-8298-1423-X   Paper/136 pages/$17.00

INTRODUCING ASIAN FEMINIST THEOLOGY
KWOK PUI-LAN

The book introduces the history, critical issues, and direction of feminist theology as a grass roots movement in Asia. Kwok Pui-Lan takes care to highlight the diversity of this broad movement, noting that not all women theologians in Asia embrace feminism. Amid a diverse range of socio-political, religiocultural, postcultural, and postcolonial contexts, this book lifts up the diversity of voices and ways of doing feminist theology while attending to women's experiences, how the Bible is interpreted, and the ways that Asian religious traditions are appropriated. It searches out a passionate, life-affirming spirituality through feminine images of God, new metaphors for Christ, and a reformulation of sin and redemption.

ISBN 0-8298-1399-3   Paper/136 pages/$17.00

INTRODUCING BODY THEOLOGY
LISA ISHERWOOD AND ELIZABETH STUART

Because Christianity asserts that God was incarnated in human form, one might expect that its theologies would be body affirming. Yet for women (and indeed also for gay men) the body has been the site for oppression. *Introducing Body Theology* offers a body-centered theology that discusses cosmology, ecology, ethics, immortality, and sexuality, in a concise introduction that proposes and encourages a positive theology of the body.

ISBN 0-8298-1375-6   Paper/168 pages/$16.95

INTRODUCING FEMINIST IMAGES OF GOD
MARY GREY

Mary Grey presents recent thinking reflecting early attempts to move beyond restrictive God language, opening up the possibilities of more inclusive ways of praying. The rich experiences of God, distinctive and diverse, are seen through the eyes of many different cultures and the women who struggle for justice. Using the figure of Sophia Wisdom as an example, Grey shows that there are many still unplumbed images of God to discover.

ISBN 0-8298-1418-3   Paper/136 pages/$17.00

INTRODUCING A PRACTICAL FEMINIST THEOLOGY OF WORSHIP
JANET WOOTTON

Only three great women-songs are retained in the Bible: Deborah's song for ordinary people, Hannah's song of triumph, and Mary's song at meeting her cousin Elizabeth. Many others, such as Miriam's song, are truncated or overshadowed by male triumphs. *Introducing a Practical Feminist Theology of Worship* begins by revealing how women have been "whispering liturgy." It then explores female images of God, discusses how worship spaces function, and offers practical suggestions for how women can use words and movements to construct authentic forms of worship.

ISBN 0-8298-1405-1   Paper/148 pages/$16.95

INTRODUCING REDEMPTION IN CHRISTIAN FEMINISM
ROSEMARY R. RUETHER

Introducing Redemption in Christian Feminism explores the dichotomy between two patterns of thinking found in Christianity: the redemption of Christ being applied to all without regard to gender, and the exclusion of women from leadership because women were created subordinate to men and because women were more culpable for sin. After examining these two patterns, Ruether examines some key theological themes: Christology, the self, the cross, and eschatology.

ISBN 0-8298-1382-9   Paper/136 pages/$15.95

INTRODUCING THEALOGY: DISCOURSE ON THE GODDESS
MELISSA RAPHAEL

Introducing Thealogy provides an accessible but critical introduction to the relationship of religion, theo/alogy, and gender especially as these concepts unfold in the revival of Goddess religion among feminists in Europe, North America, and Australasia. Raphael focuses on the boundaries of that broad movement, what is meant by the Goddess, theology in history and ethics, the political implications of the movement, and how it relates to feminist witchcraft.

ISBN 0-8298-1379-9   Paper/184 pages/$17.95

To order call 1-800-537-3394
fax 216-736-2206
or visit our Web site at pilgrimpress.com
Prices do not include shipping and handling.
Prices subject to change without notice.